ORGANIC GARDENING
■ Step by Step to Growing Success ■

Dave Pike

CROWOOD GARDENING GUIDES

First published in 1990 by
The Crowood Press Ltd
Gipsy Lane
Swindon
Wiltshire
SN2 6DQ

British Library Cataloguing in Publication Data

Pike, Dave
    Organic gardening.
    I. Gardens. Organic cultivation
    I. Title
    635.0484

ISBN 1 85223 465 2

Photographs by Dave Pike
Line illustrations by Claire Upsdale-Jones

Typeset by Avonset, Midsomer Norton, Bath
Printed and bound by Times Offset Pte. Ltd, Singapore

Contents

 # Introduction

My aim in writing this book has not been simply to provide a guide to growing organic vegetables, which is perhaps what first springs to mind when organic gardening is mentioned. Rather, I have set out to tackle gardening in all its aspects – lawns, flower-beds, shrubs, fruit trees *and* vegetables – from the organic point of view. After all, raising organic vegetables next to a lawn which you maintain with factory-made chemical fertilisers and weedkillers, or beside fruit trees which you have sprayed with insecticides, hardly constitutes true organic gardening.

Nor has my purpose been to write an all-encompassing gardening manual like so many others – covering everything from sowing seeds to growing ornamental plants to producing edible crops – but with the adjective 'organic' attached to it. Instead, I have aimed to cover some of the techniques, or as I prefer to call them, 'hidden working practices' – involving a knowledge of drainage, soils, rootstocks, flowering times, immune or disease-resistant varieties, life cycles of pests, and diseases – which help to bring about a natural balance in the garden without the aid of chemicals.

It has to be said that creating an ideal environment for organic cultivation is far from easy, given our already polluted planet. Somewhere along the chain of organic growing there is always a weak link. For example, although farmyard manure is an organic substance, it may also be chemically contaminated depending on the type of feed given to the animals producing it. The grass they eat may have been sprayed with chemical fertilisers, the water they drink may be polluted with chemicals. Indeed, the very rainwater that falls on our organic crops may be affected by emissions from factory chimneys, not to mention the effects of nuclear dumping at sea. Once the oceans gave us clean seaweed and fish by-products, but how certain of their purity can we be today? And even were we to establish a complete organic programme, problems might still arise from neighbours using non-organic methods. . .

Whatever the difficulties, however, increased awareness of ecological issues, together with the realisation that we are what we eat, have led to an upsurge of interest in organic gardening. We now know that some practices which we have taken for granted, such as the burning of stubble and the use of petrol-driven mowers and cultivators, should be avoided in order to slow down the 'greenhouse effect'. In our own small way, and however tiny our gardens, with careful planning and forethought, and by taking selective advantage of the latest modern research, products and techniques, we can not only derive great satisfaction from growing flowers, fruit and vegetables, but also play our part in preserving the natural balance of our immediate environment.

A final word about the book: I have adopted a step-by-step approach, and it would therefore be advisable to read through chapter by chapter from the beginning.

CHAPTER 1

Soils

Soil is one of the main considerations when planning the organic garden. It may seem in this chapter as if I am jumping backward and forward between natural and man-made soil conditions: my reason for doing so is to show how the soil works with nature and how we have to try as far as possible to re-create natural conditions. Results depend on hard work in the form of double digging, and the application of an organic soil conditioner.

It is important for the soil to be free from pests, disease and certain forms of weeds, and from chemical contamination. At the same time we need to maintain a healthy population of algae, fungi, microscopic organisms (bacteria) and soil-working insects such as worms and beetles. These are immensely helpful in mixing the organic substances into the soil particles and in helping the aeration of the soil.

The soil will also need a good drainage system; time must be spent studying the soil of your growing section, looking for wet areas, deciding which way the ground slopes and ascertaining whether the area for growing your organic crops will need a simple soakaway or a complete drainage system (see Chapter 3). To ignore a drainage problem may necessitate a rethink of the growing area at a later stage, causing a loss of time and possibly of crops.

The best time to study the wet section of the growing areas is during late autumn, winter and early spring. Look out for puddles as well as for dry areas, and also test the pH (see page 10) once during the late autumn and then again in the early spring, making notes of any changes.

If you have just moved to new surroundings

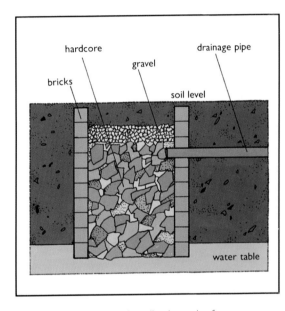

Fig 1 Soakaway, the main collecting point for excess water.

and are therefore unfamiliar with the soil, you should not rush out and start planting straightaway. It is far better to wait, if possible for one year, maintaining the area and keeping it free from weeds during this study period. Record and plan your growing area very carefully: one year of waiting may save you many years of hard work.

The ideal soil for growing crops is made up of different-sized particles: clay (less than 0.002mm), silt (0.002–0.02mm) and sand (0.02–0.2mm). Stones and gravel range from 2mm downward. For soil to have good drainage and aeration, all these particle sizes and their different shapes and shapes are required.

SOIL TEXTURE

This relates to the different types of soil particles such as sand, grit, clay and humus; to the size of the particles, and to the amounts of each type of particle contained in that class of soil. In other words, if a soil has a high sand content it is said to be a sandy soil; if it has a high percentage of clay it is called a clay soil. This latter type is hard to dig (heavy) and in most cases poorly drained; a sandy soil, on the other hand, will be open, allowing movement of air and water. A soil which has a very high percentage of sand will need extra feeding and organic substances to retain moisture.

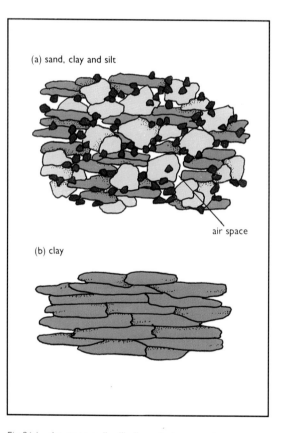

Fig 2(a) An open soil will allow drainage and a good supply of air.
Fig 2(b) A clay soil hinders drainage and air flow.

An instant way to identify your soil is to feel it. If you pick up a handful of moist earth and are able to break it up into crumbs which feel gritty, you have a sandy soil. A silky feel to the soil will indicate a high proportion of silt. If the earth remains in a solid lump which feels wet and sticky, then this is a clay soil. To produce a soil with a good crumb structure, clay, silt, sand and humus particles all need to be present in the correct balance.

Clay

In most cases clay will feel heavy, wet and sticky, and it will often be hard work. It is sometimes called a 'cold' soil because it takes a long time to warm up in the spring. Clay belongs to a group of sticky paste substances called 'colloids' and its small, closely stacked particles leave very few and very small spaces in between, thus restricting the flow of air and water. The spaces can become waterlogged and plants may die off in such airless conditions. However, although clay can cause serious drainage problems and can be difficult to break up, it nevertheless plays an important part in forming a tilth (see overleaf, Crumb Structure) and is essential for base exchange.

Base Exchange

Base exchange is very important. When soluble fertilizers are used, the bases in the soil help to prevent the nutrients from being washed away (leached) in the drainage system. The core of the soil particle is surrounded by a sticky paste which holds certain bases, such as hydrogen, calcium, potassium, magnesium and sodium. These bases are then able to exchange with bases found in the fertilizer, helping them to cling on to the soil particles.

Silt

Silt comes from very small grain particles of silica and from the larger particles of the very fine silicates. Only when they have blended with clay, sand and humus and gone through further weathering are silt particles useful in a soil. Like the very small particles of clay, silt will hinder the movement of air and water through the soil.

Sand

Sand particles can be either fine or coarse. The ideal soil for organic crops is one with a high percentage of fine sand, which is able to hold more moisture than a coarse sand. If not supplied with large amounts of organic matter, the latter will dry out very quickly and offer little in the way of plant nutrients. However, coarse sand plays a very important part in the movement of air and water through the soil.

Crumb Structure

As we have seen, the ideal soil needs to allow for a good flow of air and water, and to provide a combination of particles which will break up easily into a crumbly structure. These crumbs or aggregates are held together by the colloidal substance found in clay and humus particles. Because there are different particle sizes when sand, silt, clay and humus are combined, the crumbs will not become compacted but will allow movement of air and water. The root systems of the crops grown in such a soil will also be able to penetrate easily. In this way a tilth, or soil suitable for plant growth, is formed.

Organic Matter

Under natural growing conditions, such as in a forest or woodland, or on grassland or moorland, organic matter originates from the autumn fall of leaves and needles, rotting plants, dead micro-organisms and smaller animal life, and droppings from living animals. Some of this matter is already in a well-rotted state while other organic substances are just starting their breaking-down cycle. There are two cycles which help with the growing of crops: the carbon cycle and the nitrogen cycle.

OTHER CONSIDERATIONS

Carbon cycle (See Fig 5)

Carbon is never destroyed, but is continuously recycled, working in the soil, in the cells of plants or in the atmosphere (as carbon dioxide, CO_2). Carbon dioxide plays a very important part in the planet's plant life by assisting in the process of photosynthesis – the production of sugar and starches in the green plant – (see Fig 4). However, as man continues to burn fossil fuels, more and more carbon dioxide is being released into the atmosphere. This is producing what scientists call the 'greenhouse effect', where the carbon dioxide traps the sun's radiated heat and thereby increases the temperature of the earth's surface. Forests around the world which act as converters of carbon dioxide are also being destroyed, and hence the natural balance is being upset.

Fig 3 A balanced combination of different-sized particles makes an ideal soil.

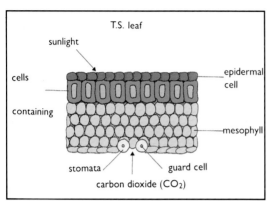

Fig 4   Cell system of a leaf.

Nitrogen cycle (See Fig 5)

Nitrogen is an essential element in all living material. The nitrogen cycle is a circulation of nitrogen in the form of ammonia, nitrites and then nitrates. Firstly, ammonia is formed when plant and animal remains start to break down. The second stage is the formation of nitrites when bacteria called *Nitrosomonas* oxidise the ammonia. Nitrites are very harmful to crops, and the third stage of the breakdown, when bacteria called *Nitrobacter* change the nitrites into nitrates for absorption into the plant's roots, is therefore very important.

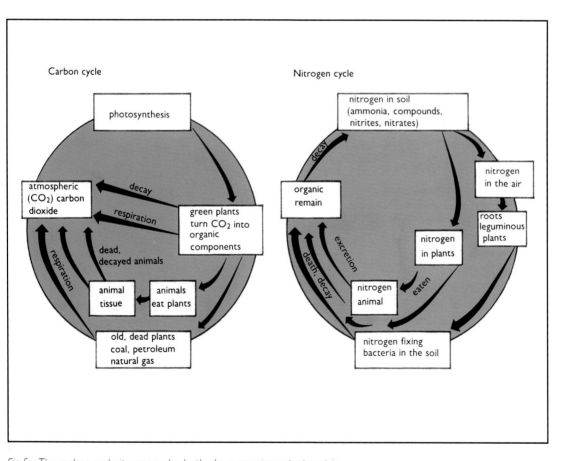

Fig 5   The carbon and nitrogen cycles both play a very important part in organic cultivation and the welfare of our plant and planet.

Up to this point I have been talking about soil in the abstract, uncultivated, under natural growing conditions such as a forest, woodland, grassland etc, where nature provides the materials, but in order to get the best from our soil, we have to apply organic matter in the form of decaying old and new plant matter and animal droppings. This can be applied in two ways: either dug back into the soil in the form of a green manure (see page 19), or worked into the soil in a man-made form, broken down on the compost heap. But before we go any further, we need to consider the temperature and the lime content of the soil or compost heap.

Temperature

The breakdown of organic substances will not take place at low temperatures; a temperature above 5°C (40°F) is needed. A 'cold' soil (one which takes a long time to warm up in the spring) will take longer to break down organic matter than a soil which is classed as warm. In Chapter 3 we will look at drainage, one of the most important aspects of trying to maintain a warm soil.

Lime content

Organic substances will break down much faster in a chalky soil, or a soil which has had lime applied to increase the pH to around 6.5 to 7.0, or a compost heap where lime has been added.
    Two of the several types of lime are:
1. Hydrated lime (calcium hydroxide, $Ca(OH)_2$). This form of lime is produced from quicklime, is quick-acting and stores for long periods.
2. Carbonate of lime (calcium carbonate $CaCO_3$). There are two forms: 'ground chalk' and 'ground limestone'.
    Lime is essential for the well-being of soil organisms such as bacteria and for preventing nutrients such as potassium, calcium and magnesium from becoming soluble and being washed away. Some plants, known as lime-hating plants, thrive in an acid soil. These include rhododendrons and the majority of heathers. The reason for this is that trace elements such as iron, boron and manganese become insoluble in a soil with a high lime content, making them impossible for the plant to take in.

pH level

The pH scale (measuring 1–14) is used to measure acidity, the term pH referring to the hydrogen ion concentration in a soil. A pH of 7 is neutral, numbers below 7 indicate an acid soil and numbers above 7 mean it is alkaline. Testing can be carried out electrometrically or with chemical kits such as a BDH soil indicator (mainly used by professionals). Smaller pH testing kits are available from garden centres. The kit works on a system of dyes as follows:

Colour	pH number
Red	4
Orange	5
Yellow	6
Green	7
Blue	8

Fig 6 A kit to test the pH levels as shown will take away the need for guesswork.

Before lime is added, the pH of the soil should first be tested to determine the amount required. A pH level of 6.5 upwards indicates that lime is not required, but a soil with a pH of 6.0 or lower will need liming. Over-liming will cause deficiency and exhaustion of organic matter. The amount of lime applied to the soil will be governed not only by the pH level, but also by the type of soil – clay, sandy, etc – and by the form of lime used. I would suggest that you take guidance from your local garden centre, explaining the type of soil and your general growing conditions, and then follow their recommendations together with the information provided on the bag containing the lime. If you live in a chalky area there may be no need to add lime.

Calcareous Soils

The term 'calcareous' refers to a soil which is found overlying three different forms of material: chalk, limestone and marl. Chalk consists of nearly pure calcium carbonate, containing minute fossil fragments of marine organisms. Chalk is very porous on its own and may cause problems in hot, dry weather. It is also termed a 'hungry' soil and may require more feeding due to the loss of the trace elements iron, boron and manganese. The reason for these losses is that the organic matter will oxidise more quickly in a calcareous soil than in a neutral soil. Although chalk will dry out very quickly in hot weather, when mixed with clay it produces a very sticky combination.

Limestone, on the other hand, tends to be very stony and, like larger particles such as gravel, is free draining. This will again cause problems in dry weather. Limestone is even more of a hungry soil than chalk.

Marl is a form of limestone and can be found mixed in clay or sand. When mixed with sand it is usually open and workable, but when mixed with clay it produces wet, heavy soil that is hard to work.

Fig 7 Soil over chalk bed rock.

A LIST OF PLANTS AND THEIR PREFERRED SOIL TYPE

The list below is a guide: there are exceptions to the rules, where plants flourish in pockets of alien soil, and no distinction is made, for instance, between light and heavy clay soils. However, the list will give you a general understanding of the type of plant suitable for your garden.

Clay Soils

Trees

Acer (Maple)
Aesculus (Horse chestnut)
Alnus (Alder)
Carpinus (Hornbeam)
Cedrus (Cedar)
Chamaecyparis (Cypress)
Crataegus (Hawthorn)
X Cupressocyparis
Cupressus (Cypress)
Eucalyptus (Gum)
Fagus (Beech)
Fraxinus (Ash)
Ilex (Holly)
Laburnum

11

Fig 8 Colourful foliage is an extra bonus, as with this form of holly.

Chamaecyparis
Chimonanthus
  (Winter sweet)
Choisya ternata
Cistus (Sun rose)
Colutea (Bladder
  senna)
Convolvulus
Cornus (Dogwood)
Corylus (Hazel)
Cotinus (Smoke tree)
Cotoneaster
Crataegus
Cytisus (Broom)
Deutzia
Elaeagnus
Escallonia
Euonymus

Euphorbia
Forsythia
Fuchsia
Genista (Rock broom)
Hamamelis (Witch
  hazel)
Helianthemum (Rock
  rose)
Helichrysum
Hibiscus syriacus
Hippophae (Sea
  buckthorn)
Hypericum (St John's
  wort)
Hyssopus
Ilex (Holly)
Jasminum (Jasmine)
Juniperus (Juniper)

Libocedrus
Magnolia (some
  varieties)
Malus (Flowering
  crabs)
Picea (Spruce)
Pinus (Pine)
Populus (Poplar)

Prunus (Cherry)
Quercus (Oak)
Salix (Willow)
Sorbus (Mountain ash)
Taxus (Yew)
Thuja (Arbor vitae)
Tilia (Lime)
Ulmus (Elm)

Shrubs

Abelia
Aethionema
Aralis elata
Aronia (Chokeberry)
Aucuba japonica
Berberis (Barberry)
Buddleia (Butterfly
  bush)

Buxus (Box)
Caryopteris
Ceanothus
  (Californian lilac)
Ceratostigma
  (Plumbago)
Chaenomeles
  (Japonica)

Fig 9 The smoke bush (Cotinus) is mainly grown as a shrub, but can make a small, attractive tree bearing flowers which resemble smoke when viewed at a distance.

Fig 10   The colourful Euonymus foliage is ideal for ground cover.

Kerria (Jew's mallow)
Lavendula (Lavender)
Ligustrum (Privet)
Lonicera
   (Honeysuckle)
Lupinus
Magnolia (some
   varieties)
Mahonia
Osmanthus

Penstemon
Philadelphus (Mock
   orange)
Potentilla
Pyracantha (Firethorn)
Rhus (Sumach)
Ribes (Currants/
   gooseberries)
Rosa (Rose)

Rosmarinus
   (Rosemary)
Salvia
Sambucus (Elder)
Santolina (Cotton
   lavender)
Senecio greyi
Skimmia
Spartium (Spanish
   broom)

Spiraea (Shrubby
   meadowsweet)
Symphoricarpos
Syringa (Lilac)
Taxus (Yew)
Thuja (Arbor vitae)
Thymus
Viburnum
Weigela

Flowering Plants

Acantholimon
Acanthus
Achillea
Alchemilla
Allium
Althaea
Alyssum
Anaphalis
Anchusa
Anemone
Anthemis
Aquilegia
Arabis
Arctotis
Armeria (Thrift)
Artemisia
Aster (Michaelmas
    daisy)
Astilbe
Aubretia
Bellis
Bergenia
Campanula
Catananche
Centaurea
Centranthus
Cheiranthus
Chicory
Chrysanthemum
Clarkia
Clematis
Convallaria
Convolvulus
Coreopsis
Cosmos
Dahlia
Delphinium
Dianthus (Pinks)
Dicentra
Dimorphotheca
Doronicum (Leopard's
    bane)
Echinops
Echium

Erigeron
Erinus
Eryngium
Erysium
Euphorbia
Filipendula
Gaillardia
Gazania
Geranium
Geum
Godetia
Gypsophila
Helenium
Helianthus
Helichrysum
Helleborus
Hemerocallis
Hesperis
Heuchera
Hosta
Hypericum
Iberis
Iris
Kniphofia
Lathyrus
Lavatera
Linaria
Linum
Lobelia
Lunaria
Lupinus
Lychnis (Campion)
Malcolmia
Malope
Matthiola
Mesembryanthemum
Myosotis
Nemesia
Nemophila
Nepeta (Catmint)
Nigella
Paeonia
Papaver
Penstemon

Petunia
Phlox
Physostegia
Polemonium
Polygonatum
Polygonum
Potentilla
Primula (some
    varieties)
Pulmonaria
Pulsatilla
Pyrethrum
Ranunculus
Rudbeckia
Salvia
Sanguisorba
Saxifraga
Scabiosa

Sedum (Stonecrop)
Sempervivum
Sidalcea
Silene
Solidago
Stachys
Thalictrum (Meadow
    rue)
Tradescantia
Trollius
X Venidio-arctotis
Verbascum
Verbena
Veronica
Vinca
Viola
Zinnia

Bulbs

Allium
Anemone
Chionodoxa
Colchicum
Crocosmia
Crocus
Cyclamen
Endymion
Eranthis
Galanthus

Gladiolus
Hyacinthus
Iris
Leucojum
Lilium (some varieties)
Muscari
Narcissus
Scilla
Tulipa

Climbers

Actindia
Abelia
Ampelopsis
Clematis
Forsythia (suspensa)
Hedera
Humulus
Hydrangea (Petiotaris)
Jasminum
Lathyrus

Lonicera
Passiflora
Parthenocissus
Pileostegia
Polygonum
Rubus
Schisandra
Trachelospermum
vitis
Wisteria

Fig II   Winter-flowering jasmine exposes flowers on naked branches during the cold spells of winter.

Sandy Soils

Trees

Acer negundo
Aesculus (Horse chestnut)
Ailanthus altissima (Tree of heaven)
Arctostaphyllos
Betula (Birch)
Castanea (Chestnut)
Cercis (Judas tree)
Gleditsia

Ilex aquifolium (Holly)
Magnolia
Nyssa
Platanus (Plane)
Populus (Poplar)
Populus canescens
Populus tremula
Robinia (False acacia)
Ulmus pumila

Shrubs

Acer ginnala
Arctostaphyllos
Aucuba (Laurel)
Berberis (Barberry)
Calluna (Ling)
Camellia
Caragana (Pea tree)
Cercis (Judas tree)
Cistus (Sun rose)
Colutea arborescens
Cotoneaster
Cytissus (Broom)
Daboecia (Irish heath)
Elaeagnus augustifolia
Elaeagnus commutata
Enkianthus
Ephedra
Erica (Heath)

Eucryphia
Fothergilla
Gaultheria
Genista (Rock broom)
Hakea microcarpa
Halimodendron helodendron
Helianthemum (Rock rose)
Hibiscus
Hypericum (St. John's wort)
Ilex crenata
Indigofera
Kalmia (American laurel)
Kerria japonica
Lapageria

Fig 12   Heathers which thrive on acid soil make excellent ground cover.

Lavandula (Lavender)
Ligustrum amurense
  (Privet)
Lonicera
  (Honeysuckle)
Lycium barbarum

Magnolia
Menziesia
Pernettya mucronata
Pernettya prostrata
Philesia
Phyllodoce

Physocarpus
  opulifolius
Rhododendron
Rosa pimpinellifolio
Salix caprea
Salix cinerea oleifolia

Salix repens
Tamarix (Tamarisk)
Ulex (Gorse)
Vaccinium
Viburnum lentago
Wisteria

Fig 13   The cherry tree (Prunus) also offers attractive autumn foliage plus
shiny bark and colourful flowers.

Flowering Plants

Armeria (Thrift)
Dianthus (Pinks)
Doronicum (Leopard's bane)
Gentiana
Lithospermum

Lychnis (Campion)
Nepeta (Catmint)
Santolina
Sedum (Stonecrop)
Thalictrum (Meadow rue)

Conifers

Cupressus glabra
Juniperus (Juniper)

Pinus (Pine)

Bulbs

Lilium

Nomocharis

Chalky Soils

Trees

Acer (Maple)
Aesculus (Horse chestnut)
Carpinus (Hornbeam)
Cercis (Judas tree)
Crataegus oxyacantha
Fagus (Beech)
Fraxinus (Ash)
Malus (Flowering crabs)

Morus nigra
Populus (Poplar)
Prunus (Cherry)
Salix (Willow)
Sorbus (Mountain ash)
Tilia (Lime)
Ulmus (Elm)

Shrubs

Aucuba japonica
Baccharis
Berberis (Barberry)

Buddleia (Butterfly bush)
Buxus (Box)

Caragana arborescens
Ceanothus (Californian lilac)
Cistus (Sun rose)
Colutea (Bladder senna)
Cornus mas
Cotoneaster
Crataegus
Cytissus (Broom)
Deutzia
Dipelta floribunda
Elaeagnus
Euonymus
Forsythia
Fuchsia
Genista (Rock broom)
Hebe (Veronica)
Hibiscus
Hypericum (St. John's wort)
Kerria (Jew's mallow)
Laurus nobilis
Ligustrum (Privet)
Lonicera (Honeysuckle)
Mahonia
Olearia

Philadelphus (Mock orange)
Phillyrea
Photinia
Potentilla
Prunus (Cherry tree)
Pyracantha (Firethorn)
Rhus (Sumach)
Ribes (Currants/gooseberries)
Rosa (Rose)
Rosmarinus (Rosemary
Rubus (Bramble)
Sambucus (Elder)
Sarcococca (Christmas box)
Senecio
Spartium (Spanish broom)
Spiraea (Shrubby meadowsweet)
Stachyurus
Symphoricarpos
Syringa (Lilac)
Vinca (Periwinkle)
Weigela
Yucca

Conifers

Cedrus (Cedar)
Juniperus (Juniper)
Pinus (Pine)

Taxus (Yew)
Thuja (Arbor vitae)
Thujopsis

Evergreens

Ilex (Holly)

Taxus (Yew)

CHAPTER 2

Organic Matter

Through a combination of factors such as drainage, air flow, temperature, pH, micro-organisms and organic matter, a system is built up for breaking down organic matter such as plant remains into a substance called humus.

Humus

Many people confuse organic matter with humus. In fact, humus derives from organic matter. It is black in colour and contains particles smaller than those of clay. Unlike clay, silt, sand and gravel it cannot be separated from the rest of the soil; instead it acts like a glue which sticks to sand particles and plays a very important part in the formation of a crumb structure. Humus also has the ability to exchange a wide range of plant foods, including nitrogen, and it serves as a working and living area for the micro-organisms in the soil. If those countries of the world subject to high temperatures and sandy soils were to recycle organic substances in the soil to produce humus, instead of using chemical fertilisers which can destroy it, dust-bowls might be prevented.

There are two ways in which organic matter decomposes and the type of soil plays a very important part in that process. In a poorly drained or waterlogged soil, the supply of oxygen is restricted and sometimes even completely missing. Under these anaerobic conditions, therefore, organic matter decays to produce a different form of humus such as peat.

FORMS OF ORGANIC MATTER

Below I have listed various forms of organic matter. The first can be used for the compost heap as well as dug into the soil. Other forms of organic matter for digging into the soil fresh are dealt with in the green manure section. Unfortunately, although these forms of organic matter are very beneficial to the soil, they are very low in nutrient content, and this is one of the reasons why those looking for mass production of crops turn to chemical feeds.

Farmyard manure (F.Y.M.) This can be a mixture of materials such as cow, horse and pig dung, straw, and straw used as bedding, which in

Fig 14 Animal bedding.

18

most cases contains urine and dung left by the animal using the bedding. There is a difference between the various animal manures.

Cow/pig manure This is termed a cold or wet manure because of its high moisture content. Although this can be to your advantage if you have a sandy soil, decomposition may be slower in clay because of its cooler soil temperature and higher moisture content. Having a clay soil myself, I prefer to use cow manure, which is slightly dryer than pig manure.

Horse manure Because it produces heat when breaking down, this is termed a hot manure. It is very good for the production of warm soils (hot beds).

Poultry manure This is very rich and will need storing and drying before use; I have often seen crop roots burnt because gardeners have used fresh poultry manure.

Straw This is used more as a soil conditioner and may be used on its own or in a compost heap with other materials, as described in the section on compost heaps in Chapter 3 (page 30). Other factors which govern the quality and the organic or non-organic levels of farmyard manure are the kind of food which the animal eats; the treatment given to the feed before and during storage; and the surrounding environment, where chemicals such as weedkillers and fertilisers, and even radiation fall-out, have an effect, which in turn is passed on to the soil and the root system of our crops.

Spent mushroom compost Cheaper to buy than peat and can be used both on the compost heap and as a soil conditioner.

Green manure This term basically refers to crops like clover or alfalfa which are grown in order to be worked back into the soil before crops are planted. This then breaks down, either helping to condition the soil or feed it with

Fig 15 Animal bedding with a mixture of horse manure.

nutrients such as nitrogen. Other substances, such as seaweed, are also termed green manures; although this type of organic matter is not sown as a crop I include it here because it is dug in when fresh.

Nitrogen Fixation

To understand why we use green manure, we must first appreciate that bacteria – or nitrogen fixation bacteria – live not only in the soil, but also in swellings (nodules) found on the roots of leguminous plants. These bacteria are able to use the atmospheric nitrogen and turn it into an organic form. Whilst the plant is living, the bacteria and the plant form a symbiotic relationship, with the plant providing forms of organic carbon compounds like sugar, and in return the bacteria offering nitrogen to the plant.

Organic matter can be divided into two main forms: eating crops, sown in the spring or late summer, which are then dug into the soil after cropping, and plants which are grown during rest periods purely to be dug into the soil in autumn in order to prepare it for a main crop.

19

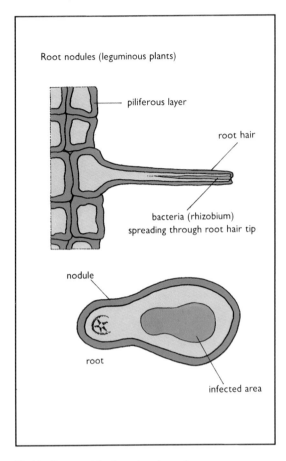

Root nodules (leguminous plants)

piliferous layer

root hair

bacteria (rhizobium)
spreading through root hair tip

nodule

root

infected area

Fig 16   Root nodules found on leguminous plants such as clover are a good source of organic nitrogen.

Main Crop or Spring Sowing

Broad bean   The roots of this plant offer nitrogen when worked back into the soil after being cropped.

Peas   Rich in nitrogen fixation.

Clover   Also rich in nitrogen fixation. Red clover is one of the favourites and is sown in the late summer as well as the spring. Dig in 2–3 weeks before planting crops.

Rye –Secale cereale   Good for working back into the soil in the spring after being sown in late summer. Seed can be collected and used the following year.

Seaweed   Unlike dung and straw, seaweed is best dug into the soil when fresh. It contains no weed and few if any pests or diseases.

Organic Matter for Preparation or Rest Periods

Alfalfa   Although best suited to the larger garden, there is no reason why you should not try alfalfa for one season as it offers nitrogen to the soil. Sow in spring at 14-16g per sq metre and dig into the soil in the autumn.

Buckwheat (*Fagopyrum esculentum*)
Sow in late spring and then work back into the soil in the autumn.

Mustard (*Sinapsis alba*)   Used for new growing areas or those taking a year's rest. Sow in the spring or summer and then work back into the soil before flowering.

Other Forms of Organic Matter

Spent hops   Very good as a soil conditioner, but contain very little nutrient. Apply at the rate of 300–500g per sq metre.

Cattle cake   The dust from this, which contains a percentage of nitrogen, can be applied at the rate of 270g per sq metre.

Feathers   These also contain nitrogen which is made available when worked into the soil. Apply at the rate of 270g per sq metre.

Shoddy   This is the left-overs from the textile industry such as wool, cloth and silk, but care should be taken that these items have not been contaminated with oil or chemical dyes (*see* Suspect organic waste).

Suspect organic waste Although many forms of household and commercial waste may be added to the compost heap, care should be taken to avoid those contaminated by chemicals and metals. Therefore by all means compost spent vegetable peelings, etc, but take out tin cans, oily rags, paper covered in paint, etc.

CONCENTRATED ORGANIC MANURES

Animal remains such as bones and blood, plant remains and the ash from burnt wood, will form concentrated organic manures. Unlike straw, spent mushroom compost, etc, which add body and improve the physical condition of the soil, these concentrates offer more in the way of food. The term 'food' is used loosely at this stage and the substances listed below should be classed as manure until they are applied to the soil. Before they are made available to the root system they have to go through the process of being changed into nitrates. There are two forms, quick- and slow-release concentrated organic manures. The speed with which nutrients are made available depends on the type of organic material containing them, also soil temperature and drainage, air flow, pH levels, amounts of organic matter, and bacterial activity.

A slow-release manure can be applied a few weeks before planting and will then gradually

Top dressing

Spread substance by hand.

Lightly hoe into soil.

Fig 17   Spread the top dressing by hand, then work into the top layer with a hoe.

release nutrients over a period of several months – in some cases years – as with the coarse 'hoof and horn' concentrates. With a quick-release concentrate, crops should in most cases have been planted, although dried blood, for example, will take 7–10 days to break down.

Top-dressing This refers to the application of either a concentrated manure/feed, or a mulch, on the soil's surface. In the case of the manure/feed, a light hoeing to work it into the surface layer of the soil is beneficial, but a mulch is simply spread over the ground.

Quick-acting Concentrates

Dried blood The amounts of nitrogen and phosphoric acid plus the rates at which the contents should be applied are normally given on the bag if this is purchased from the garden centre, but as a general guide dried blood contains 7–14 per cent nitrogen and 1–2 per cent phosphoric acid. Apply the blood in the form of a top-dressing at 7–30g per sq metre, depending on the type of soil and the amounts of nutrients already in it.

Fish guano This is made from fish after the oil has been taken away. It contains 5–9 per cent of nitrogen and the same amount of phosphoric acid. These nutrients are not only made available quickly, they also last for a long time, but they do need to be applied in advance and in a partly broken-down state, otherwise they may burn the root system. When applied as a base dressing (i.e. dug in) the rate is 130–140g per sq metre.

Wood ash This contains mineral salts. Only clean, non-diseased and non-contaminated wood (that is, which is not covered with oil, paint, etc) should be used. Also, the initial lighting material must be clean paper; petrol, paraffin and rubber tyres should not be used. Quick acting, wood ash supplies 1–5 per cent potash plus other minerals. Apply at the rate of 130–250g per sq metre.

Fig 18 Burning wood will produce a supply of potash.

Slow-release Concentrates

Hoof and horn When purchasing hoof and horn from your local garden centre, ask for the fine powder form used for potting rather than the coarse gritty powder which may take several years to break down. Hoof and horn supplies approximately 7–14 per cent of nitrogen. Apply as a base dressing before planting, at the rate of 60–250g per sq metre.

Steamed bonemeal Boiled bones ground to a fine powder contain 20–30 per cent phosphoric acid. Apply at the rate of 65–250g per sq metre.

All these organic substances can be used both as soil conditioners and as suppliers of small amounts of essential nutrients. Unfortunately the operative word is 'small', because vast quantities of organic matter are needed to supply the same amount of nutrients as a single bag of chemical fertilizer, especially when the soil is not particularly ideal.

MAJOR AND TRACE ELEMENTS

Major elements are needed in large amounts and act upon the main growing sections of the plant, whereas trace elements work in smaller amounts and act as a catalyst, speeding up the reaction of the major elements.

Major Elements

Although water and air which pass through the soil may not seem a source of food, they are both classed as major elements. This is due to the supply of carbon which is found in air, hydrogen found in water, and oxygen found in both air and water. Both air and water are brought to the soil by rain, or by artificial watering on a regular basis during the growing season. Therefore, by providing your soil with an open structure which allows air to pass through freely together with the water, you are making it receptive to the first major elements.

Deficiency and Cause

To list all the deficiencies and causes would be impossible in this book, and in any case other factors may affect the colour or markings of a plant. Only through time and experience will you begin to understand each deficiency.

N.P.K. These letters stand for nitrogen, phosphorus and potassium, which are the next three major elements and are applied by feeding the soil with organic matter.

Nitrogen (N) The plant extracts the available nitrogen from the soil for most of its major growth processes such as the stem and leaves; nitrogen also helps to give the plant its rich green colour by assisting in the formation of chlorophyll (the green colouring-matter found in plants). Over-feeding your plants with nitrogen, especially towards the autumn and winter, will produce weak, sappy growth which could be damaged by cold weather, strong winds and pests.

Nitrogen deficiency Stunted growth, off-yellow/green in colour.
Cause Lack of organic matter, a cold, water-logged or poorly drained soil, pH level too low, and low bacterial action.

Phosphorus (P) Plays an important role in the formation of cells in the plant, particularly in root formation. Later helps to ripen and mature the plant.
Phosphorus deficiency Dull greenish in colour, poor root growth.
Cause Lack of organic matter to produce humus, pH too low, acid or clay soils, cold, water-logged and poorly drained soils, and low bacterial action.

Potassium (K) Helps to build up resistance to disease which in turn helps to regulate the sap flow. Potassium is particularly necessary with crops which store sugar and starch, such as the carrot.
Potassium deficiency Leaves turn a blue-green colour, and brown scorch marks appear on the tips of shoots and in the leaf margins.
Cause Free-draining sandy soils and chalk soils, lack of organic matter.

Calcium (Ca) Plays an important part in the growing tips above the ground and in the tips of roots below ground, plus helping in the formation of cells and strengthening the plant's structure.
Deficiency Poor root growth, the tips of leaves unsightly.
Cause Acid soils, pH too low, lack of organic matter.

Magnesium (Mg) Magnesium helps to form chlorophyll and works with phosphorus, which in turn assists in seed formation.
Deficiency Yellowy/green colour found in the older leaves of the plant, affecting the younger leaves at a later stage (this is called 'chlorosis').
Cause Sandy soil, lack of organic matter.

Sulphur (S) Sulphurous elements in the soil aid protein formation and the production of oils found in the plant.
Deficiency Unlikely to be found in British soils.

Trace Elements

Manganese (Mn) Helps with the formation of chlorophyll.
Deficiency Yellow-green to yellow leaves.
Cause Over-limed or chalky soils, too much organic activity.

Iron (Fe) Plays an important part in the forming of chlorophyll.
Deficiency Yellow leaves and other parts of the plant (the green sections) containing chlorophyll.
Cause Chalk soil, lime soil, over-liming, and any other conditions where iron becomes insoluble.

Boron (B) Works closely with calcium and is influential in the absorption of the major element.
Deficiency Diseases such as canker.
Cause Open, sandy soils.

Molybdenum (Mo) Plays a very important role in nitrogen fixation.
Deficiency Diseases such as whiptail.
Cause Acid soils.

To summarize, we need a balance of soil particles such as clay, sand, etc, plus a balance of organic material and the right conditions such as drainage, temperature, pH level and bacteria; we also need a good supply of major and trace elements which come from minerals already found in the soil or from the break down of organic matter. Organic matter contains far less of these than artificially produced chemical fertilizers, and you may have to resign yourself to plants which are perhaps a little less than they might be in appearance, given artificial supplements.

CHAPTER 3

Soil Drainage

The first step towards putting the last two chapters into practice and beginning cultivation of your soil is to determine your soil type and its pH level. Then look for drainage problems. If you have a free-draining, sandy soil you may need to slow down the loss of moisture by applying organic matter at a later stage, but for the moment let us concentrate on those soils with poor drainage and air flow. Unless excess water can escape, the soil will be waterlogged and airless, therefore ways of improving the drainage or forming a drainage system must be found.

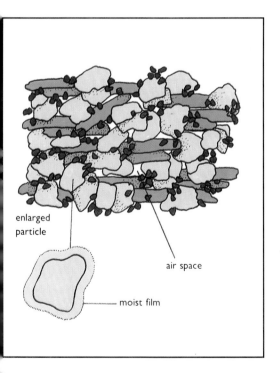

Fig 19 Soil particle enlarged.

Before starting to improve or build the drainage system we need to take a quick look at the way in which water moves and is lost in the soil.

WATER IN THE SOIL

There is always water in the soil even in a hot, dry summer, and to understand this we must again look into the chemical reaction within the soil. These chemical reactions are so strong that water is held in the soil against the pull of gravity, sticking to the soil particles (hygroscopic action) and thus being made unavailable to the root growing in the soil. Soils such as peat or those with too much organic matter are good examples of this. It is one reason why over-feeding with organic matter is not advisable: again, it is a question of balance. The second way water is held in the soil is by capillary action, where the moisture is held around the soil particle as shown in Fig 19.

Water Table

This is the upper level of excess water that has drained through the soil and become trapped in permeable rocks beneath. The level of the water table varies with the amount of rainfall, being lower in the summer and higher in winter.

It is true to say that a clay soil is capable of a higher water table than a sandy soil. The water table must be taken into consideration when building a drainage system. Those living close to rivers, streams, etc may find that the water table is high for most of the year, even − in some

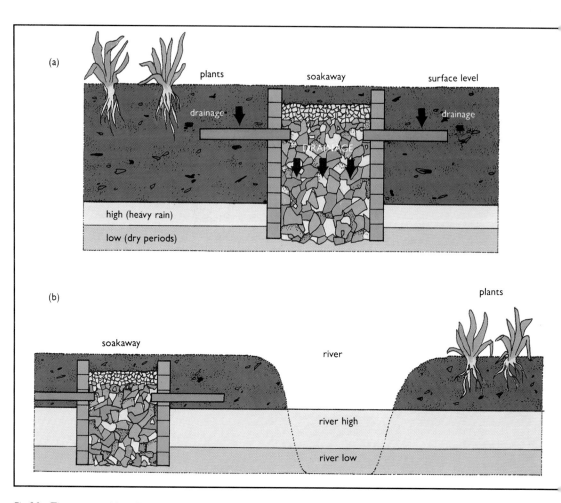

Fig 20   The water table will govern the depth of the soakaway.

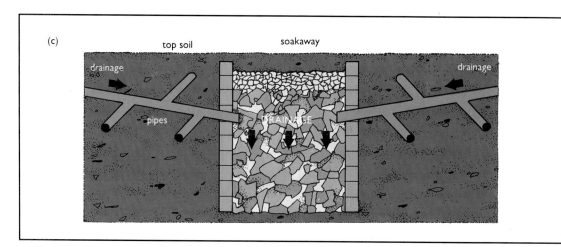

Fig 21   Hardcore used to fill the soakaway will ensure good drainage.

extreme cases – throughout the whole year, and these will always have a drainage problem. If this is the case then raised beds may be your answer (see Chapter 4, page 38).

Soakaway

You may find that the levels in your garden all run the same way and therefore water collects in one area. This is the ideal position for the soakaway, but if for some other reason the water lies in several areas, a drainage system such as pipes may be called for. Either way, it is much safer for the non-pollution of general public waterways if the drainage pipes are fed into a soakaway rather than tapping into the main drainage system through the side of a manhole cover or ditch, stream or river – indeed, if you did this you might be breaking the law.

Building a Soakaway

When you have found the area where the water stays the longest, or the lowest point in the garden, mark an area 1–2 metres square, then dig down as far as possible or to the water table. This may be 1–2 metres, the deeper the better.

NOTE It is advisable when digging a deep hole to:

1) Shore up the side walls to stop them from collapsing on top of you.
2) Have someone close at hand in case of an emergency.
3) Contact the gas and electricity people to find out if there are any pipes or wires in the area, and whilst digging keep looking for them, as they may not always be shown on plans.
4) Keep all children away from the hole and secure the area if left overnight.
5) Remember the water table: if the hole continuously fills with water, stop digging.

The next step is to place bricks up all four sides of the hole as shown in Fig 20. If a pipe drainage

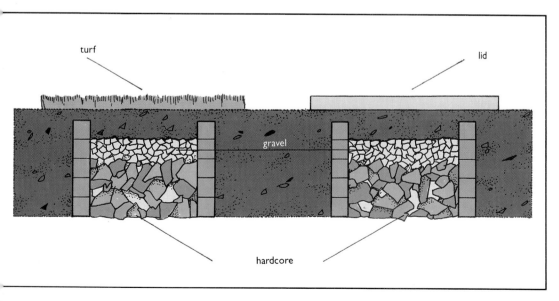

Fig 22   Two ways of covering the soakaway.

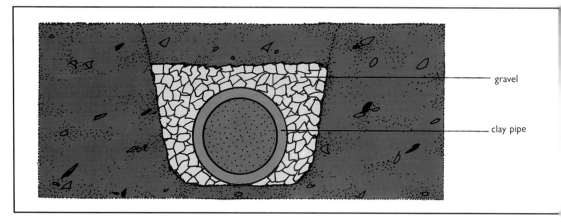

Fig 23   Clay drainage pipe.

system is used, place the pipe – or pipes, if more than one drain is used – in between the bricks, as shown in Fig 20. Fill in the hole with broken bricks, large gravel and stones (but not very fine sand), as shown in Fig 21. On top of the rubble place a large-size pea grit, and fill to the top of the hole with top soil. Grass can be sown or turf laid over the top, or the area can be covered with a lid as shown in Fig 22.

Drainage pipes   The old-style drainage pipes are made of a clay substance which is very porous, but at the same time when linked together they will make a channel to carry the water to the soakaway. Modern pipe lines are usually made of plastic, but will do the same job. This form of drainage system is the ideal rather than just a soakaway, but it may be costly, and providing all levels run to the soakaway, it may not be necessary.

To lay the drainage pipes you must first mark out the area to be dug. If the soakaway is at one end of the garden then one main drain with several minor drains should be sufficient, as shown in Fig 24. If the soakaway is in the centre of the garden then two, three or four main drains with minor drains can be used.

After you have marked out the areas, dig to a depth of approximately 0.6 – 1 metre for the main drain and slightly less for the minor drains. The depth is determined by the type of soil; for example, a clay soil should have pipes closer to the surface as well as being closer together, whereas a sandy soil should have the pipes deeper and wider apart. Both main and minor drains should have a slight fall towards the soakaway – in other words, the water will run downhill from the highest point of the garden to the soakaway as shown in Fig 25.

When you have finished digging the trenches place the pipes in the trench on the angle (slight fall, approximately 1 metre to every 60 metres) and then fill in the trench with large pea grit as shown in Fig 23 and finish off with top soil. The surface area may either be grassed over or left covered with soil, but remember to draw a plan for future reference should repairs need to be carried out, or to avoid breaking pipes when planting.

Putting a drainage system into your garden may seem like a lot of heavy, back-breaking work, especially if the garden is new and full of builders' rubble, which is usually compacted. However, the benefits will be worth the effort, for the drainage system will improve the soil by:

1) Draining away excess water.
2) Improving the air flow through the soil.
3) Creating a warmer soil.
4) Allowing organic matter to break down more quickly.

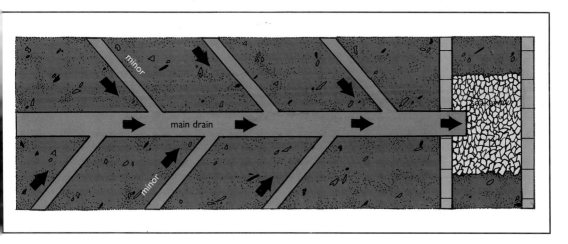

Fig 24   The minor drains take the water to the main drain which leads to the soakaway.

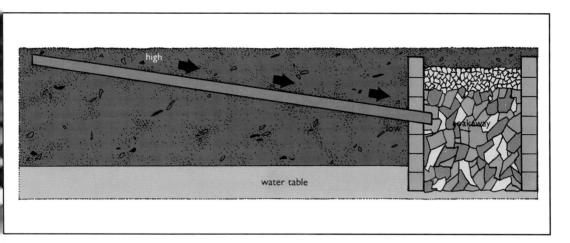

Fig 25   All pipework should slope towards the soakaway.

LOSS OF WATER IN THE SOIL

During a hot, dry summer less water is available for the plants' needs, therefore it is important that a watering programme is followed. There are several ways in which water is lost in the soil:

1) Capillary action and hygroscopic action.
2) Percolation, when water drains through to the water table leaving the plant with very little moisture, and removing nutrients from the soil, washing them down to the water table.
3) Moisture taken by the plant through a form of pump action (transpiration). This is when the plant loses moisture through its foliage. It is affected by wind speeds, temperature, etc.
4) Moisture lost to unwanted plants such as weeds.
5) Evaporation, when moisture is lost during hot, dry weather.

COMPOSTING AND STORAGE

Once the drainage problems have been sorted out it is time to consider the storage of organic matter and the compost heap. First, let us take a look at storage, which is not to be confused with the normal compost heap which needs a good air flow and moisture. Here, we are looking at fresh, raw material which needs storing before digging into the soil or adding to the compost heap.

The reason we store organic matter such as cow, horse, pig manure and straw is because if used fresh it would probably burn the root system of the plant, and, in the case of straw, it is easier to apply when in a partly decomposed state. Therefore storage for periods of between 6 – 12 months is necessary.

Compost/Storing F.Y.M.

F.Y.M., or farmyard manure, is the term for cow, pig, and horse manure and also included is the straw bedding containing urine.

NOTE Remember, the organic quality of animal manure depends on the type of feed and the way it was processed before the animals ate it. Any chemicals in it will pass through into the animals' manure. Grass, too, may be suspect if it has been treated with chemical fertilizers, and atmospheric pollution should also be taken into consideration.

Stacking Fresh, Raw Material Heaps to Avoid Losses

Without air Before digging the manure into the soil it will need storing in a bay. First find a clean area and lay a concrete base, then build a three-sided wooden or brick construction on top (wooden sides should be without gaps in between each board). A removable slanting roof is a good idea, but black plastic may be used to keep down costs (*see* Fig 29). Avoid stacking the manure in heaps: it is important that air is not allowed to pass too freely through the heap as it would cause the loss of important nutrients such as ammonia, and you will therefore need to tread down the top of the manure after stacking it into the bay.

Without large amounts of moisture
Nitrogen is lost from the heap if moisture such as heavy rain is allowed to pass through, therefore a roof is necessary. However, the heap should never be allowed to become too dry or too hot, which would damage organic matter such as straw.

Remember, some types of manure contain more moisture than others, thus a heap of horse manure which contains small amounts of moisture will warm up more quickly than cow or pig manure which contains large amounts of moisture. Poultry manure, on the other hand, is very hot and rich and great care should be taken when using this. When storing poultry manure, the heap should contain alternate layers of manure and soil, and it is even more important that air should be excluded than for F.Y.M.

Compost/Storing Straw

When straw is used as a soil conditioner it should be in a partly decomposed condition in order to mix with the soil particles. Therefore, as with the F.Y.M., it will need storing and composting, but unlike the F.Y.M., straw needs a good supply of air and moisture, but should not be too wet. Dry straw is totally unsuitable for composting, and either straw soaked with water (without becoming waterlogged) or, better still, animal bedding covered in urine should be used. Either way, a form of liquid manure such as the sludge found around cattle pens should be applied to the heap to help speed up the rotting processes. Soil and animal manure should be added to each layer of the heap to encourage bacteria, and for these to survive we need the correct pH. Therefore, chalk should also be added to the heap, as shown in Fig 26.

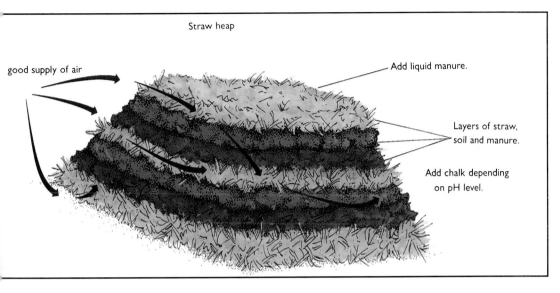

good supply of air

Straw heap

Add liquid manure.

Layers of straw,
soil and manure.

Add chalk depending
on pH level.

Fig 26   Straw and liquid and horse manure combined make an ideal
organic fertilizer.

Grass cuttings

Grass cuttings taken from the lawn can either be stored in the same way as straw, or composted with other waste such as potato peelings, etc. The point to remember when composting grass is to use only cuttings taken from untreated (chemical-free) lawns (*see* Chapter 6). Using grass cuttings as a form of mulch is not such a good idea as one might think, mainly because of the release of ammonia which can burn surface roots.

The Compost Heap

From now on the compost heap will play a major role in your organic garden as it will be the main source of nutrients. Therefore a constant supply of raw organic material will be needed, but it should be remembered that over-feeding can be as dangerous as under-feeding. At the same time soil-testing for the levels of nitrogen, etc should be carried out as often as possible. Finding good untreated organic material is a far from easy task, but you may have a friendly farmer,

Fig 27   Household refuse such as cabbage leaves and potato peelings make an ideal compost.

31

mushroom grower or local stables willing to help with the supply of such important fuel. In most cases it will come down to rethinking the so-called 'rubbish' which, until the 'green' era revived the practice of our grandparents' days, was thrown away. Items such as cabbage leaves, potato peelings, onion skins, leftover fish, and others too numerous to list, can all by recycled if we take the time to save them.

Building the Compost Heap

The first thing we need is a clean area to build the compost heap and, since it may look unsightly and will definitely give off an odour, it should be sited away from the house (and the neighbours) if possible, and screened from view by some form of hedge, wall or fence. For very small gardens there are small units made of plastic or wire mesh which may be purchased from the

Tumble compost bin

Fig 28   A tumble compost bin will take the hard work out of turning the compost.

Fig 29   A compost bay is easy to make from old wooden boards.

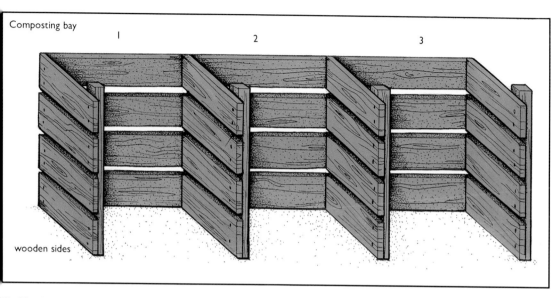

Fig 30 A three-way compost system.

garden centre. The compost heap may be built by forming a mound of layers like the straw heap; or by building bays such as that shown in Fig 29. A three-bay system can also be used, as shown in Fig 30.

Composting in layers Mark out a clean area 1–2sq metres (the size will depend on the space available), then place your first layer, building up to about 30cm in thickness. This layer should contain straw bedding, soil, household waste and some form of F.Y.M. Add animal urine if possible, tread the layer, and water without waterlogging. On top of this, spread a thin layer of soil, then continue to build the heap (which should have slanting sides) until you have reached the desired height, which can be anywhere between 1.5 to 2.5 metres. Lime should be added to the heap if you used a soil with a pH below 7, and watering should be carried out every two weeks, or more frequently during hot weather. Turning the heap every 5–6 weeks can be heavy work, but is most important in helping to speed up the rotting process by maintaining a good air supply, and it exchanges the material on the outside of the heap

with the material in the centre. Anyone with a bad back would be well advised to use the bay system instead, which tends to involve smaller amounts and therefore is easier to work with.

Composting using bays Mark out a clean area. A concrete base is helpful in keeping the area clean and providing a solid base on which to build, but is not essential. Start by building the three bays as shown in Fig 30, the first for storing and collecting organic matter, the second for the breakdown stage of organic matter, and the third for material ready for use. Place removable boards with air spaces in between them at the front of each bay to stop the material from falling out. Build the heap inside the first bay with a layer of organic material such as grass cuttings, cabbage leaves, onion skins and potato peelings plus a form of F.Y.M. such as straw bedding containing cow- or horse-manure and urine. Tread the compost and then cover with a thin layer of soil (disease- and pest-free). Add lime if the soil has a pH level below 7 and then water the heap, continuing to build the layers until you have reached the desired height. Turning the heap every 5–6 weeks will maintain the air supply and help to speed up decomposition, ensuring that the material on the outside of the heap is moved into the centre.

EARTHWORMS

Organic gardening is by no means easy work, therefore help in any form is most welcome. Assistance can come from weather conditions such as frost, or the soil population. We have already looked at bacteria and their beneficial effect, so now let us take a look at those larger organisms such as worms.

The earthworm is an excellent helper, mixing the organic matter with the soil particles in all levels from the topsoil down to the upper layers of subsoil, and it should be encouraged, but certain conditions are needed to maintain a healthy population of our friendly worker. These are: an

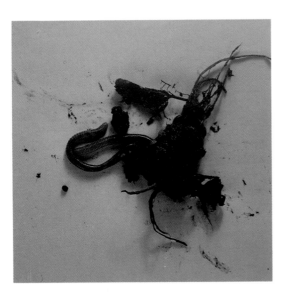

Fig 31 The earthworm is the organic gardener's best friend.

open, warm soil with an abundance of organic matter to eat and pass through their bodies (earthworms do not eat living plants), and a pH level of between 6.5–7. In the first stages of development when your soil conditions may not be favourable to the earthworm, a container with good ventilation designed for the reproduction of worms is a good idea. The container is filled with a suitable compost such as a mixture of well rotted straw and F.Y.M., sand and clean garden soil (pest- and disease-free), with a pH level of around 7. Earthworms can then be added to the compost and allowed to breed. The worms are released back into the soil along with the rich ingredients which have been left in their breeding boxes.

Earthworm's Life Cycle (Annelida– Oligochaeta)

Earthworms work mainly in the top 50–60cm layer of the soil, and in good fertile soils can exceed several million per hectare in population. However, during cold weather they tend to penetrate deeper into the soil. They are hermaphrodites, that is, they are classed as being both male and female. Mating, which produces around 25–30 eggs, may take place under the soil as well as on the soil surface. These eggs hatch after a month or two into juvenile worms which reach their adult stage within a year.

Enchytraeid Worms

These are smaller than the earthworm and thrive on rotting organic matter such as leaf mould and other forms of manure.

There are, too, insects which are helpful in mixing the soil, but which also attack roots, seeds and earthworms. They are dealt with in Chapter 11

CHAPTER 4

Cultivation of Soils

Soil cultivation can basically be broken down into three types: the cultivation of a clay soil, a sandy soil and a calcareous soil (that is, over chalk or limestone). Although there are soils in between and overlapping these categories, our main aim is to try to change each of these soil conditions as far as possible in order to create a uniform soil which will react with organic matter and provide a good drainage system with a healthy air supply.

Soil Colour and Temperature

A light colour will reflect the sun's rays whereas a dark colour will absorb heat; therefore a soil

Fig 32   A dark brown or black soil will hold the heat and therefore warm up more quickly than those which are lighter in colour.

which is light in colour will take longer to warm up, whilst a darker coloured one will warm up quickly. Thus the uniform soil we are looking for should be a dark brown to black in colour.

Aspect   The direction in which the garden faces will play an important part in the warming of the soil. For instance, if the soil area is south facing – and especially if it is on a slope – it will warm up more quickly than a soil area facing north.

CULTIVATION OF A CLAY SOIL

The main problem with a clay soil, as we have seen, is its lack of drainage. Having installed a drainage system, we now need to improve the soil itself.

To break down and change clay soil takes time and patience, and it is no good thinking you can rush out and throw a bag of sand or peat over it and expect it to change overnight. You will first need to double dig the area, which will break up the top section of the subsoil and help with the drainage and air flow lower down in the soil. At the same time you will need to concentrate on the surface layer. Frost will play a major part in helping to form a tilth in the spring and therefore the digging should be carried out during late autumn and the earth left in large lumps. Before starting to dig you will also need to apply organic matter and some form of open material as shown below.

Applying organic matter   Since clay soil has such a high moisture content, horse manure which is low in moisture and classed as a hot, dry

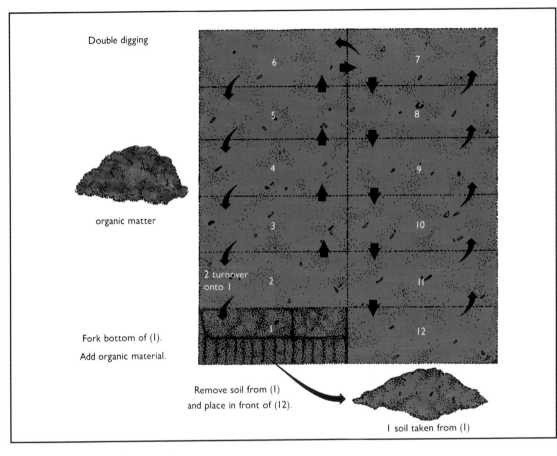

Double digging

organic matter

2 turnover
onto 1

Fork bottom of (1).
Add organic material.

Remove soil from (1)
and place in front of (12).

1 soil taken from (1)

Fig 33   Double digging plan.

manure is far more suited than the wetter cow or pig manure. Straw that has been stored mixed in with the horse manure will work as a soil conditioner. Although we need to keep up the supply of organic matter by applying a mulch throughout the year, the organic matter is only dug into the soil once a year when autumn digging takes place. Apply at the rate of 5–7kg per sq metre. Soil testing for the amounts of nitrogen, phosphates and potash should be carried out on a regular basis to avoid overfeeding the soil with organic matter and in order to maintain a balance.

Applying an open material   Coarse sand and grit (lime free – do not use builders' sand) must be applied and mixed with all levels of the soil. This will eventually supply us with the dif-

Fig 34   Frost helps to break down heavy soil.

36

Fig 35 Coarse sand and grit will help with drainage and all soils should contain some particles of this size.

ferent sized particles which are so important for drainage and air flow.

Applying lime First carry out a test for the pH level, which will give you an indication of whether the soil needs lime and if so, how much. A pH level above 6.5 should not need lime. Ground limestone is the most suitable for clay soils. It should be applied in the autumn, the rate being governed by the pH level. For example, a pH of 6 will need between 0.75–0.85kg per sq metre.

CULTIVATION OF A SANDY SOIL

Since the problem with a sandy soil is that it drains only too well, resulting in loss of moisture and nutrients from the soil, it is therefore necessary to apply large amounts of cow and pig manure with their high moisture content.

Drainage Sandy soil should be free from surface drainage problems.

Green manure This should be applied every year to form the type of balanced soil we are looking for, and again time will play its part. Instead of rushing into sowing flowers, it would be far better to wait for a period of a year or so and apply an organic substance to the soil. Therefore a green crop over the next two years, such a leguminous or lupin crop with their nitrogen fixing root nodules, will work as a soil conditioner, feed and improve the moisture-holding content of the soil.

Potash In the majority of sandy soils this is in short supply. Wood ash – try to obtain it from clean, non-diseased wood – can be applied at the rate of approximately 130–250g per sq metre.

Lime Because of its free drainage, sandy soil will have most of the calcium washed out of it and therefore it may become very acid. The type of lime best suited to a sandy soil is ground chalk, which works slowly in the breakdown of organic matter. The amount to be applied will depend on the pH level of your soil (*see* pH level, page 10).

Time of cultivation Cultivation of sandy soil can take place throughout the year, even in cold and wet weather, but because the soil warms up quickly and is also quick to dry out after a heavy rainfall, I would still favour the early spring and late autumn.

CULTIVATION OF A CALCAREOUS SOIL

Calcareous soil can be broken down into three sections: chalk, limestone and clay marls. The clay marls can be treated in the same way as a clay soil (*see* page 35), but the chalk and limestone cultivation is as follows.

37

CULTIVATION OF A CHALK SOIL

Digging to break up the chalk, and incorporating organic matter (which tends to be used up very quickly because the high pH level boosts the action of bacteria) should be carried out during late autumn.

To avoid the formation of a crust a light forking with a small border fork, or hoeing, can take place from spring to autumn. Covering the surface with a layer of well-rotted mulch such as F.Y.M., spent mushroom compost or tree bark free from pest and disease will also help to stop a crust forming.

Drainage   There should not be too much of a problem with surface drainage.

Green manure   A green manure can be very beneficial to a chalk soil, as it can be to a sandy soil.

Lime   There should be no need to lime a chalk soil.

Potassium   There is a tendency for potassium to be in short supply in the chalk soil, therefore potash produced from burnt wood should be applied at the rate of 130–250g per sq metre.

CULTIVATION OF A LIMESTONE SOIL

This is basically the same as the cultivation of a chalk soil.

RAISED BEDS

The raised bed is a useful method of cultivation in areas with very high water tables or for people unable to take on heavy digging. Not only is it good for drainage, but it also allows you to create a new topsoil level by buying in clean pest-, disease- and weed-free soil with a balanced pH level, and if the raised bed is built on top of a soil that has been worked for several years, the old topsoil section will then become a cultivated subsoil.

Another point in favour of using raised beds is that there will be greater depth for the roots to penetrate. The raised bed can be simply constructed by adding soil on top of the existing soil, but you will be forever building up the sides. Planks of wood (never use railway sleepers since they have been coated with preservatives which may escape during hot weather) can be erected, but the trouble with wood is that it needs replacing regularly or treating with a preservative, and is therefore drawing us away from our organic goals. My preference is for a simple dry stone wall construction which can then be filled with clean soil.

Building a Raised Bed

Step one   Although raised beds will help with the drainage problem, it is still important that you form a main drainage system, as shown in Chapter 3, if possible, and general cultivation as already described is recommended before building the raised beds. Only then can you be sure of a good drainage system and a cultivated subsoil for deep-rooting plants such as apple trees.

Step two   Start by marking out the growing areas, which can be small or large depending on the space available and the type of crop or plant to be grown. When growing vegetables and following a crop rotation as practised by conventional growers, a large area will be needed, but there is no reason why three smaller beds as opposed to one large area cannot be used. Then work out the height of the sides of the raised bed, and this will be governed by the water table. The higher the water table the higher the sides of the raised bed should be, and consideration should be given to the type of crop and the amount of root run (depth of root) needed.

Fig 36 A raised bed can help in overcoming drainage problems.

Material I have found that sandstone will crumble when hit by frost, therefore the hard Cotswold flat stone is the ideal type to look for.

WEED CONTROL

A weed is a plant growing in the wrong place, and although we only think of the type of weed found in the lawn, flower-bed and vegetable patch, the term can also relate to shrubs and trees, etc. Therefore we first have to decide which is the major crop or crops being grown in a certain area, and all other plants can be termed weeds. Most surface weeds can either be pulled out by hand or destroyed by hoeing; however, there are some varieties which either have a long tap root such as the dandelion, or a rhizome, like couch grass.

If parts of the rhizome are left in the soil they will continue to grow, and therefore digging rather than hand weeding or hoeing is more suitable for keeping this type of weed under control.

Weed Control on Cultivated Land

Most people either acquire an established garden or a new one which has had some form of cultivation, in that topsoil has been laid, and therefore weed control does not call for the drastic measures needed for uncultivated land.

Weed control on cultivated land can be divided into three sections: vegetable patches, flower-beds and herbaceous borders; tree and shrub areas; and grass areas (this will be covered in Chapter 6).

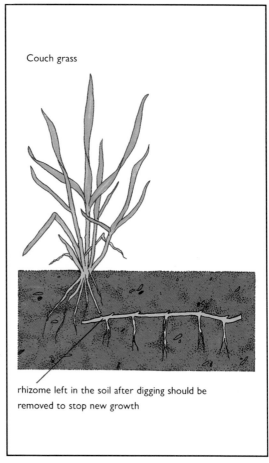

Couch grass

rhizome left in the soil after digging should be removed to stop new growth

Fig 37 All rhizomes should be removed to control couch grass.

Fig 38   It is advisable to leave a new garden barren over the winter period so that the soil and any drainage problems can be investigated.

Fig 39   Two hoes used in the control of weeds.

Vegetable Patches, etc

Remove all deep-rooted and rhizome weeds during the autumn digging, hand weed and hoe surface roots throughout the rest of the year.

Tree and Shrub Beds

Weeding a tree and shrub bed can be carried out in three different ways:

1) Hand weeding and hoeing throughout the growing season.

2) Covering the bed during the growing season with a mulch such as clean (i.e. pest- and disease-free) tree bark.

3) Using black plastic.

Mulching   The mulch, whether clean tree bark, spent mushroom compost, or decomposed straw, will help to control weeds by

Fig 40   The weeds here have been controlled by hoeing.

locking out the light and thus preventing photo-synthesis; the weeds then either become leggy and weak, or fail to grow at all. Although some seeds will inevitably find their way into the mulch and germinate, these can be removed very easily by hand. Spread a 5cm layer over the surface of the soil, covering the complete area. Two other bonus points with a mulch are that it will help to stop the surface of the soil from drying out too quickly in hot weather, and it will break down and work its way into the soil, acting as a soil conditioner.

Black plastic   Black plastic is ideal for the long-term growing areas, effectively stopping the light from reaching the weeds. A mulch such as tree bark is needed to cover up the unsightly plastic, and although the odd weed may grow in the mulch layer, it can easily be removed by hand. Lay the plastic as follows:

Fig 41   Planting through black polythene will help in the control of weeds.

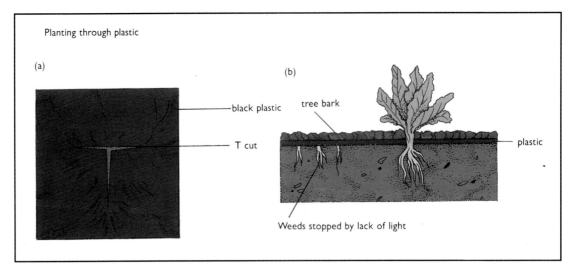

Fig 42   Black plastic will help control weeds by stopping the light from reaching them.

Step one   The soil should be cultivated in advance and brought as close as possible to the balanced ideal described earlier. A fairly thick grade plastic is better than a thin grade. Before covering the growing area with the plastic, lightly fork over the surface of the soil, then roll out the plastic and pin down the ends, either with pegs or under the top layer of stone if used on a raised bed. Then 'T' cuts can be made and holes dug ready for the plants to be inserted.

Step two   Secure the root system of the plants into the soil, pull the plastic right up to the stem then cover it with a layer of tree bark.

Weed Control on Uncultivated Land

More drastic measures are necessary on land which has had no cultivation of any kind. An uncultivated piece of land has its advantages as well as its disadvantages. It may be a long, back-breaking task to clear the area of weeds and brushwood, etc without the aid of chemicals before bringing it under cultivation, but if the land has not been chemically treated then there should be a good balance between pests and predators. The only safe way to clear the surface of the soil without destroying the balance is by hand, and even then you should first study the life cycles of the pests and predators, looking at the type of plant they use to breed on, and it may be useful to leave a small section uncultivated to allow the balance to continue.

Start by deciding on those plants you wish to keep and those you will destroy. Cut all growth down to ground level (non-petrol machines should be used if possible), then rake the area and collect all the cuttings into one heap, sorting out what can be composted and what cannot. The material cut back can be spread over the area as a form of mulch, but if you follow this practice avoid weed seeds germinating and causing the same problem all over again. A heavy grade black polythene is then laid and secured over the complete area to stop the light from reaching those plants left in the soil. The polythene is left until such time as the plants under it have died back. The area is then cultivated as described previously.

Fig 43 An uncultivated area can be left to attract beneficial insects.

Stubble Burning and Clearing Overgrown Areas

Stubble burning is a practice carried out by many farmers. However, conservation groups have repeatedly pointed out the deleterious effect of fire and smoke on wildlife and the environment, and the law takes a stern stand on the danger of burning fields close to public roads.

CHAPTER 5

Lawns

It is as important to apply organic techniques to the grass areas as it is to the vegetable or fruit-growing areas, and problems such as weeds and moss should be eradicated without the aid of chemicals, using such methods of hand cultivation as spiking, scarifying and boxing off the grass cuttings. Clover can be used as a feed, and worm casts mixed with horticultural sand spread as a top-dressing. This practice will not produce the ideal 'bowling green' lawn, but you will at least have a grass area free from contamination. Again, it is a question of balance: if you provide the best conditions possible, less time will be spent on problem control.

MOWERS

Electric or push mowers which provide a system for collecting the grass cuttings should be used rather than the petrol mower. The old-style push mower is ideal for small gardens, it will give you more exercise and is completely free from fumes, petrol and oil leaks. But for those who prefer the easy way or have a larger garden, the electric mower is more practical. Before using an electric mower, read through the instructions on how to fit the plug, where to place the lead when mowing (such as over your shoulder to avoid cutting through the cable), and never use electric

Fig 44 Push or electric mowers are more in keeping with the organic theme than those which require petrol.

Fig 45 The cylinder mower cuts rather than tears as a cylinder passes across a bottom blade.

mowers in wet weather. Long trousers and protective boots should be worn, whilst gloves and protective eye glasses are necessary under certain conditions, such as when using electric trimmers. I prefer to use the type of mower with several blades which cut across a bottom blade rather than the rotary mower.

Box off

This is a term used for collecting the grass cuttings in the box fitted to the front of the mower. Seeds from any weeds growing in the grass will be collected at the same time.

Cutting Times and Heights

Ornamental lawns can be cut three times a week, except during drought periods where once every two weeks usually works, with the first cut of the season on a high setting (topping the grass) and then at a height of 7–12mm for the rest of the season. The coarser, more hard-wearing forms of grass should start the season with a cut at a high setting, and then be cut twice a week, except during drought periods, at a height of 12–24mm for the rest of the season. Always use a box to remove cuttings and weed seeds.

CREATING A LAWN

Drainage

Any drainage problem should be dealt with in the same way as for soils (see Chapter 3), but the difference with lawns is that further treatment can be applied every year to maintain a good drainage system, which will help to control other problems such as moss.

Soil

Once any drainage problems have been sorted out, cultivate the soil. By this I mean produce a balanced, fertile soil with plenty of soil life, including worms, with a pH level of just under 7, but not below 6.5.

The soil should be dug during the late autumn and left in large lumps for the frost to break down over the winter. Before sowing seeds in the spring, the area should be lightly forked and raked over to remove all the large stones, and then brought to a fine tilth. If the turf is to be laid in late summer (August), prepare the ground beforehand by forking and raking, working the soil to a fine tilth. Spring or August are the most suitable times providing the temperature is above 10°C (50°F), but August is generally favoured especially for seed sowing because of the temperature factor. The warm soil at this time of year will allow the root system to become established for several weeks before any winter frosts. Another good point is that fewer people are likely to walk on the lawn during the winter.

The laying of turf during the hot summer months between the end of May to July should be avoided if possible, since the rate of growth slows down at this time of year and rain and tap water may be in short supply, causing root systems to dry out very quickly and large cracks to appear between each turf as it shrinks.

Raised Bed System

Those living in an area with a high water table will find that a raised bed system will be the answer. The height will depend upon the height of the water table.

Seed or Turf?

There are two ways of starting your lawn, one from seed and the other from turf. The latter will give an instant lawn, whereas seed will take approximately six months, with the additional problem of weeds fighting for moisture and light alongside the grass. Most seeds are treated chemically with pest repellents, although it is possible to purchase untreated seed; however,

Fig 46 *A raised-bed system used on a lawn will improve drainage and help control moss.*

Fig 47 *A good base is essential when laying turf.*

you will find in most cases of turf that it has been treated and fed chemically.

Seed

If you decide on seed, March or August are the best time to sow. The type of grass should be carefully chosen: seed containing rye grass is best for a hard-wearing lawn if children are to play games on it. Choose appropriate seed for shady areas covered by overhanging foliage from trees and seed producing fine grass for an ornamental lawn. There are many mixtures available today and it is advisable to seek advice from your local garden centre, but obtaining chemically un-treated seed mixtures may be difficult. For those who do manage it, scarecrows or tinfoil on string may have to be used.

Seed List

Hard-wearing lawn A mixture of the follow-ing should be used:

    55 per cent of Chewing's Fescue
    35 per cent of New Zealand Crested Dogstail
    10 per cent of Browntop (*Agrostis tenuis*)

Sowing rate is approximately 34–36g per sq metre (*see* Fig 48).

High-quality lawn Do not be tempted to aim for this if you have children or pets. This will cause you the extra work of reinstating every year. The following mixture is suitable:

    80 per cent of Chewing's Fescue 20 per cent of Browntop (*Agrostis tenuis*)

Shaded positions

30 per cent of Browntop (*Agrostis tenuis*)
20 per cent of Fine-leaved Fescue
40 per cent of Sheep's Fescue
10 per cent of Creeping Red Fescue

Sowing Grass Seed

Step one After choosing the type of grass area best suited to your situation and position, for seeds sown in early spring, cultivate the soil in the previous autumn as described above. Then early in March, weather permitting, cultivate the soil further, bringing it to a fine tilth, at the same time using a rake to remove large stones and level the surface. Firm the soil by tramping all over the surface, pushing in the heels of your boots to fill any hollows under the surface. Rolling is not necessary and in some cases will compact the soil, forming a pan which will hinder the drainage. After you have heeled the complete area, rake and level the surface again, forming a good tilth. For seeds sown in August, cultivate the soil, remove stones, level the surface and bring the soil to a fine tilth. To sow seed in August follow the same procedure for sowing in March.

Step two Now mark the area off in rows with string, each row being a metre apart. Then sow half the recommended rate of seed down the lengths marked out and when you have finished sowing in the first direction, change the strings over and sow the rest of the seed across, as shown in Fig 48.

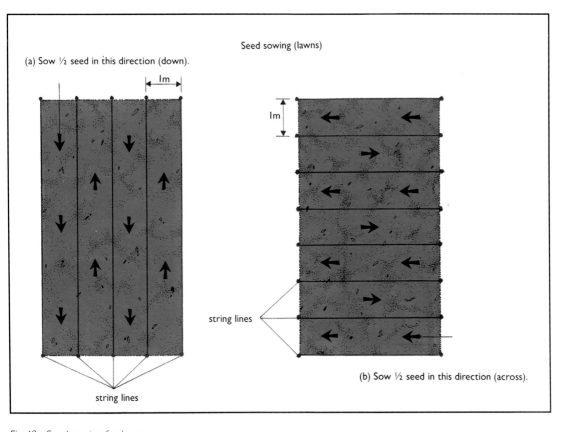

Seed sowing (lawns)

(a) Sow ½ seed in this direction (down).

Im

string lines

Im

string lines

(b) Sow ½ seed in this direction (across).

Fig 48 Seed sowing for lawns.

Fig 49 The grass box of the mower plays a very important part, not only because it collects the grass cuttings and therefore prevents the build-up of thatch, but also as it collects weed seeds.

Step three Erect objects to keep off the birds and to stop people and pets from walking over the seeded area. Once the grass has started to grow and the root system has become established (after approximately 4–6 weeks), top the grass by using a sharp-bladed mower with the blades set high and always box off the cuttings.

Turf

With all things there is good and bad, and turf is no exception. Some suppliers offer little choice and you may purchase turf complete with a full complement of weeds, but there are others who take time to cultivate their growing areas or grow on a mesh system, and these will offer a wide range of grass mixtures with very little weed. However, you will find that almost all turf sold will have been treated with chemical weedkillers and fertilizers.

Laying Turf

Step one Cultivation of the soil is basically the same as for seed sowing (*see* page 47). The dif-

ference with laying turf is that it is beneficial to apply a little extra substance such as peat to aid moisture retention around the root system. It would be far better if we found an alternative to fast diminishing supplies of valuable peat, such as very well rotted compost, but I must stress that only very well-rotted compost should be used for fear of damage to the roots if used in a partly decayed state.

Step two Only two tools are used when laying turf: a strong wooden board to walk on which at the same time helps to bed the root systems, and a sharp knife to cut and shape the turf. When laying the turf you must never allow the edges (except around the outside of the lawn) to form straight lines. Always overlap the end of each turf so that it resembles the lines in a brick wall (*see* Fig 50).

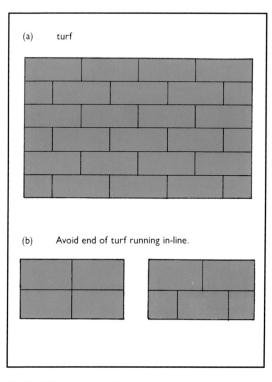

Fig 50 When laying turf, make sure each piece overlaps as shown here.

Aftercare

Water the finished job and continue to water every 2–3 days if there is no rain. Allow the grass to become established before cutting, and then cut on a high setting (topping the grass) with sharp blades and a box to collect the grass cuttings and weed seeds.

FEEDING

Although many people worry over their grass during cold spells, droughts and long periods of heavy rain, in most cases the grass will return, if lost, and often re-seeds itself. Therefore unless you are trying to produce a bowling green, feed is not as important as when growing vegetables, flowers and fruits. However, the grass will still need some form of nutrients such as nitrogen for healthy green growth, plus phosphates and potash. The nitrogen can come from allowing clover to grow in the lawn because of its nitrogen fixation, and the other two can be applied as a top-dressing in the autumn in the forms of very fine bonemeal and clean wood ash.

Fig 51 Using a fork as shown will help to improve the drainage and will aerate the soil at the same time.

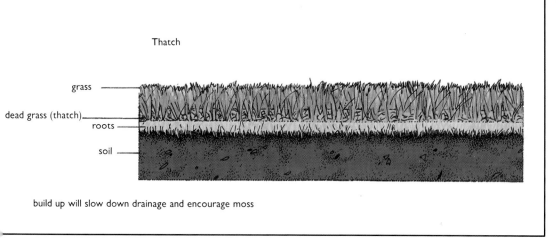

Thatch

grass

dead grass (thatch)

roots

soil

build up will slow down drainage and encourage moss

Fig 52 Thatching the lawn will hinder drainage and encourage moss.

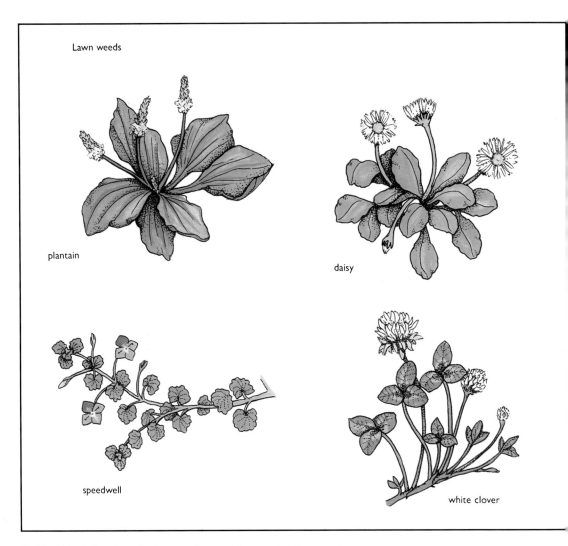

Lawn weeds

plantain

daisy

speedwell

white clover

Fig 53   Weeds found on the lawn can be troublesome, but those such as white clover can be beneficial.

MOSS CONTROL

If the drainage is working under the lawn areas, moss should not cause too much of a problem, although shaded and north-facing areas can produce moss. Therefore, the number one rule is always to ensure that there is a good working drainage system and air flow. This can be maintained by adding washed horticultural sand in the form of a top-dressing and by spiking (i.e. pushing a fork into the surface of the grass area as shown in Fig 51). The other factor which helps moss to survive is thatch. This term describes cuttings and debris which are allowed to build up around the grass stems, hindering drainage and air flow and allowing moisture to build up at the surface level, thus producing an ideal breeding ground for moss.

Fig 54   A spring box rake will easily remove the build-up of thatch on a lawn.

Scarifying The best possible method to remove this thatch organically is by the vigorous use of a rake. There are machines which will do the job, but try to avoid petrol machines if possible.

WEED CONTROL

Hand weeding should be used for deep-rooted weeds, but boxing off the grass cuttings will help to stop weeds seeding themselves.

CHAPTER 6

Seed Sowing

My intention in this chapter is not to cover seed sowing in general, but rather to suggest ways in which attacks from pest and damaging weather conditions might be avoided. Hygiene, for instance, is a very important factor in trying to control disease whilst maintaining an organic garden. Also, wherever possible use seeds which produce disease-resistant plants; this does not necessarily mean using chemically treated seed, but rather seed which has been produced through genetics.

SEED TRAY/TRANSPLANTING

Controlling pests and diseases without the aid of chemicals is the hardest task of organic growing. One way to minimize damage, although not totally fool-proof, is to sow and germinate seeds in trays or peat blocks and then transplant the seedlings into the soil at a later stage, therefore avoiding both the time when certain pests attack, and adverse weather conditions such as frost. To achieve success with this form of pest control you will need to know a little about the life cycle of the pest to be avoided. For example, the carrot fly *(Psila rosae)*, which also attacks parsley, produces two generations of larvae that eat the root system. The first generation is produced around May and June and the second during August and September. Therefore by sowing into seed trays and transplanting after the first generation has been produced, you will avoid attacks at the beginning of the year (*see also* Chapter II).

Fig 55   Seed tray and soil.

Fig 56   Sowing seeds.

germinated seeds into individual pots can be made up of horticultural sand and sterilized soil. Nutrients in the form of concentrated manures, i.e., dried blood, etc, will need to be applied, the rate depending on the size and depth of pot and the type of plant being transplanted.

Basic Soil Mixture for Seed and Transplanting

Remember that transplanting compost will need nutrients applied to it.

80% sterilized garden soil
20% horticultural sand

Hygiene Never use a seed compost more than once unless it has been sterilized by steam first, and always use a clean seed tray.

Time for Sowing

This will depend on whether the plant is hardy or half hardy. A hardy plant will tolerate lower temperatures than a half hardy one, which can only be placed outside in the soil when the fear of frosts has passed, normally around the second week of May. Hardy annual seeds used for bedding plants, for example, can be sown directly into the soil during the early part of the spring. However, I suggest that you treat all the seeds in the same way and grow them in trays rather than the soil, which will give you more control over weather conditions, enable you to move the tray away from pest-infested areas, and choose the transplanting time.

Most hardy and half hardy annuals should be sown during the early part of the spring, and this rule applies to most edible plants such as tomatoes, cabbages, peas and beans. Some, such as the groups of brassica, are sown later in the year from September to January. Some of the hardy seeds, such as tree seeds, cannot be stored for long periods, and others which can be stored will need a period of cold (called stratification) before they will germinate.

Fig 57   Cover the tray and mark the label giving the seed name and date sown.

Seed Compost

This can be an organic compost for seed sowing and transplanting, or a mixture of horticultural sand and sterilized garden soil can be used.

NOTE: A good method of sterilizing is with a commercially available sterilizing unit which looks like a bucket and stands on a container full of water. Heat is applied from the base to boil the water, the steam escapes through small holes at the bottom of the bucket and up through the soil, sterilizing it at the same time. This practice should be carried out in an open area.

One of the volcanic substances available from your local garden centre can be used as a substitute for seed compost, but you must remember that there are no nutrients in it. This is not a problem in the early stage as the seed contains forms of food in the seed coat, but this is soon used up and the plant will start to show signs of deficiencies. However, never attempt to move the seedlings before they have their first set of adult leaves (as opposed to the seed leaves, or cotyledons). A compost for transplanting the

Tree/Shrub Seed

Many tree and shrub seeds can be sown directly into the soil, although some will need a stratification period (*see* page 55). Two exceptions are the oak and the horse chestnut, which do not store very well, and therefore both of these should be collected green and sown in September or October. Seed can be collected from the wild or bought from your local garden centre. If collecting from the wild, be sure to use only seed from non-diseased trees. There are two points to remember:

1) Always ask for permission before collecting from woods, parks or private gardens.
2) Seeds taken from varieties, cultivars and hybrid trees will not always grow true to form.

Fig 58 A maple tree.

This means that if a tree has been crossed to produce a variegated leaf, in most cases its seed will produce a mixture of variegated, part-variegated and non-variegated seedlings. Only species which are true wild trees such as oak, beech, etc, will come true when grown from seed. To produce a tree identical to one which has been crossed genetically, giving it a certain colour, variegation or shape, you would need to create a cell system identical to that of the parent plant (i.e. a clone), which would entail growing from a cutting, layering, or by tissue culture rather than seed.

Time for Collecting

This depends on the type of tree or shrub and when it flowers. Shrubs such as cotoneaster and pyracantha have small white flowers and chaenomeles have large, colourful blooms, but not all tree flowers are recognisable as such, although you will find ·that most tree and shrub seeds are ready from late summer to autumn.

It is very important to collect the seeds before they go into their dormancy period, which is when nature sets a protective layer and holds the seeds back until the conditions are right for germination. The seeds should therefore be gathered before they start to ripen. If the seeds have started their dormancy period, you will need to stratify them.

Stratification

This is a process used to overcome dormancy and to do this you will need a seed tray and horticultural sand. The amounts used are one part seed to three parts sand. Mix the two together and fill a seed tray that has a depth of 7.5cm and drainage holes at the bottom.

Alternatively, spread a 2.5cm layer of peat-sand mixture over the bottom of the seed tray, then place a layer of seeds on top and cover with a second 2.5cm layer of the mixture, followed by a second layer of seed and so on until you have filled the seed tray.

Place the seed tray in the refrigerator at a temperature between 1–4°C (30–40°F) for a

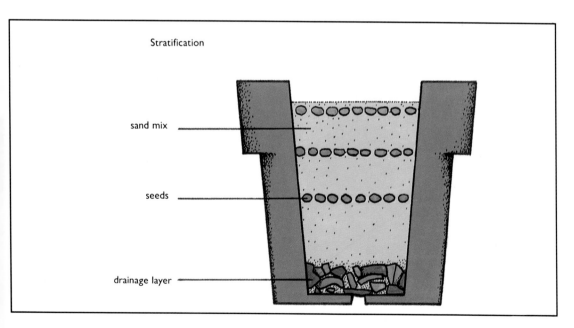

Stratification

sand mix

seeds

drainage layer

Fig 59   Some seeds will need stratifying.

period of 4–6 weeks, or outside in the coldest part of the garden, north facing if possible. Of the two, I prefer the outside position, basically because the rise and fall in temperature tends to have more effect on the seed coat. The period for leaving the seeds outside depends on the seed being used. Seeds such as those of berberis, cotoneaster, Chinese juniper, crab apple, cherry and pyracantha, all need a period of 5–6 months. All should be sown directly after the stratification period, usually around March/April.

Seed Sowing

Fill a seed tray by two-thirds and then press a firming board lightly on the surface without compacting the compost. Spread the seed evenly on the surface – this is easier with larger seeds, which can be placed rather than being scattered from the palm of your hand like small seeds. The larger seed can be covered with a layer of compost passed through a fine sieve, but with very fine seed there is no need to cover. Remember to label the seed tray with the name of the seed and the date.

Fig 60   Space the seeds evenly.

Fig 61   Space seeds evenly over the surface and lightly cover seeds with soil.

Fig 62   Label giving seed name and date sown.

Pricking Out

When the seeds have produced their first pair of adult leaves, they can be transplanted (pricked out) into individual pots. Take hold of the seedling by its seed leaves (cotyledons) to avoid damaging the stem of the plant, and with a flat dibber, push into the soil underneath the plant's root system. Ease the seedling out and transfer it to an individual pot, positioning it so that the seed leaves rest on top of the compost. Try to avoid damaging the root system and leave as much soil as possible around the roots when lifting.

Pricking out

Lift by holding seed leaves and pushing dibber under seedlings.

Fig 63 Care should be taken when pricking out so as not to damage the root system or stem of a plant.

The seeds listed below are just a few examples of sowing times – most garden centres stock seed catalogues which cover a wide range of plants. Study them and prick out those which offer some form of disease- or pest-resistance.

Seeds Sown in January – February

Rock Gardens

Aethionema	Dryas
Arenaria	Edraianthus
Armeria (Thrift)	Erinus
Aubretia	Hyacinthus
Calceolaria	Puschkinia
(Portulacaceae)	Ramonda
Cerastium (Snow-in-	Raoulia
summer)	Rhodophypoxis

Bulbs

Allium	Iris
Brodiaea	Leucojum (Snowflake)
Cardiocrinum	Muscari (Grape
Chionodoxa (Glory of	hyacinth)
the snow)	Narcissus
Crocus	Ornithogalum (Star of
Cyclamen (note –	Bethlehem)
tuberous)	Panncratium (Sea lily)
Fritillaria	Scilla
Galtonia (Summer	Sternbergia
hyacinth)	Tigridia

Herbaceous/Bedding plants

Aquilegia	Lupinus arboreus
Campanula	(Tree lupin)
(Bellflower)	Morisia
Cyananthus	Phlox
Dianthus	Phyteuma
Draba (Whitlow	Primula x variabilis
grass)	Saponaria
Leontopodium	Saxifraga
(Edelweiss)	Thymus
Limonium (Sea	Verbena
lavender)	

57

Fig 64 *Campanulas are ideal pot plants and are suitable for rock gardens.*

Shrubs

Cotula (Bladder senna)   Potentilla

Trees

Gleditsia

Seeds Sown in March – April – May

Rock Gardens

Acantholimon (Prickly heath)
Anacyclus (Mount Atlas Daisy)
Anagallis
Arabis
Asperula
Campanula (Bellflower)
Platystemon
Pulmonaria (Lungwort)

Bulbs

Techophilaea (Chilean crocus)

Herbaceous/Bedding plants

Abutilon
Acaena (New Zealand burr)
Acanthus (Bear's breeches)
Achillea (Yarrow)
Adonis
Agapanthus (African lily)
Alchemilla (Lady's mantle)
Alstromeria (Peruvian lily)
Althaea (Hollyhock)
Alyssum
Anchusa
Anthemis
Aquilegia
Arnebia
Asclepias (Milkweed)
Astrantia
Ballota
Baptisia (False indigo)
Bellis (Daisy)
Bergenia
Borago (Borage)
Brachycome
Briza
Brunnera
Calendula (Marigold)
Calluna (Ling heather)
Catananche (Cupid's dart)
Centaurea
Centranthus
Cheiranthus
Chelone
Chrysanthemum
Cladanthus
Clarkia
Coix (Grass)
Convolvulus
Coreopsis
Crepis
Cynoglossum
Delphinium
Dianthus
Dicentra
Didiscus
Digitalis (Foxglove)
Echinacea
Echinops (Globe thistle)
Epilobium (Willow herb)
Eryngium
Escholtzia
Euphorbia
Fatsia
Festuca (Grass)
Gaillardia (Blanket flower)
Galega (Goat's rue)
Geranium (Crane's bill)
Geum
Gilia
Glaucium (Horned poppy)
Godetia
Gunnera
Gypsophila
Helianthus
Helichrysum
Helictotrichon (Grass)
Heliopsis
Helipterum
Hemerocallis (Day lily)
Hepatica
Hesperis

Hyssopus
Iberis (Candytuft)
Inula
Kniphofia (Red hot poker)
Lamium (Dead nettle)
Lathyrus (Sweet pea)
Lavatera (Mallow)
Layia
Leptospermum
Leycesteria
Liatris (Blazing star, gay feather)
Limnanthes
Liriope
Linaria (Toadflax)
Linum (Flax)
Lithospermum
Lobelia
Lunaria (Honesty)
Lupinus (Lupin, lupine)
Lychnis
Lysimachia
Lythrum
Malcomia
Malope
Malva (Mallow)
Matthiola (Stock)
Mimulus (Monkey flower)
Moluccella
Morina
Myosotidium
Myosotis (Forget-me-not)
Nemophila
Nepeta
Nicandra (Shoo fly)
Nigella (Love-in-a-mist)
Oenothera
Omphalodes (Navelwort)
Ononis
Onopordum
Onosma

Origanum
Papaver
Parochetus
Pennisetum (Grass)
Penstemon
Phygelius
Pinguicula (Butterwort)
Platycodon (Balloon flower)
Podophyllum
Polemonium
Primula x variabilis
Prunella (Self-heal)
Pyrethrum
Reseda (Mignonette)
Rodgersia
Rudbeckia (Cone-flower)
Salvia
Sanguisorba
Shortia
Silene (Campion, catchfly)
Silybum
Smilacina (False Solomon's seal)
Solidago (Golden rod)
Stachys (Lamb's tongue)
Tanacetum
Teucrium
Tiarella
Thermopsis
Trachycarpus (Chusan or fan palm)
Veratrum
Verbascum (Mullein)
Verbena
Veronica (Speedwell)
Viola (Pansy)
Zantedeschia

Shrubs

Berberis (Burberry)
Buddleia (Butterfly bush)
Buxus (Box)
Callicarpa
Camellia
Carpenteria
Cassiope
Ceanothus
Celastrus (Climbing bitter sweet)
Chaenomeles (Japonica)
Chimonanthus (Winter sweet)
Cistus (Rock rose/Sun rose)
Clematis
Clethra
Cornus (Dogwood)
Corylus
Cotoneaster
Cytissus (Broom)
Daphne
Desfonainea
Dierama (Angel's fishing rod)
Dipsacus
Enkianthus
Erica (Heath, heather)
Erysimum
Escallonia
Euonymus (Spindle tree)
Fothergilla
Gaultheria
Genista (Broom)
Grevillea
Griselinia
Hamamelis (Witch hazel)
Helianthemum (Rock rose)
Hibiscus

Hydrangea
Hypericum (St John's wort)
Ilex (Holly)
Kalmia
Laurus (Bay laurel)
Ligustrum (Privet)
Lonicera (Honeysuckle)
Mahonia (Oregon grape)
Menziesia
Myrtus (Myrtle)
Nyassa
Parthenocissus (Virginia creeper)
Pernettya
Philadelphus (Mock orange)
Phlomis
Phormium
Phyllodoce
Phytolacca
Pieris
Pittosporum
Potentilla (Cinquefoil)
Pyracantha (Firethorn)
Rhododendron
Rosa (Rose)
Ruscus (Butcher's broom)
Ruta (Rue)
Sambucus (Elder)
Skimmia
Sophora (Japanese pagoda tree)
Spartium (Spanish broom)
Stranvaesia
Symphoricarpos (Snowberry)
Symplocos
Syringa (Lilac)

Fig 65 Hibiscus will make an attractive pot plant or shrub.

Ulex (Gorse)
Vaccinium (Bilberry,
   blueberry or
   cranberry)
Viburnum
Vitis (Grape vine)
Weigela

Wisteria
Yucca
Zauschneria
   (Californian fuschia)

Trees

Abies (Silver fir)
Acer (Maple)
Alnus
Araucaria (Monkey
   puzzle)

Arbutus (Strawberry
   tree)
Betula (Birch)
Carpinus (Hornbeam)
Catalpa (Indian bean)

Cedrus (Cedar)
Cercis (Judas tree)
Chamaecyparis
Crataegus (Thorn)
Cryptomeria
   (Japanese cedar)
Cupressus (True
   cypress)
Cytisus (Broom)
Davidia (Pocket
   handkerchief tree)
Embothrium
Eucalyptus (Gum tree)
Eucryphia
Fagus
Fraxinus (Ash)
Gingko (Maidenhair
   tree)
Juglans (Walnut)
Juniperus (Juniper)
Laburnum (Golden
   chain)
Larix (Larch)
Liquidambar (Sweet
   gum)
Liriodendron (Tulip
   tree)

Malus (Crab apple)
Metasequoia (Dawn
   redwood)
Nothofagus (Southern
   beech)
Paulownia
Picea (Spruce)
Pinus (Pine)
Platanus (Plane)
Prunus (Cherry)
Pseudotsuga (Douglas
   fir)
Pyrus (Pear)
Rhus (Sumach)
Robinia (False acacia)
Sequoiadendron
   (Wellingtonia)
Sorbus (Ash)
Stewartia
Taxodium (Swamp
   cypress)
Taxus (Yew)
Thuja
Thujopsis
Tsuga (Hemlock)
Zelkova (Grey bark
   elm)

Seeds Sown in September – October

Bulbs

Cardiocrinum

Herbaceous/Bedding plants

Aconitum
   (Monkshood)
Adonis
Anemone (Wild
   flower)
Angelica
Anthericum (St
   Bernard's lily)
Briza

Collinsia
Delphinium
Godetia
Lathyrus (Sweet pea)
Linaria (Toadflax)
Malcolmia
Nigella
Scabiosa (Pincushion
   flower)

Trees

Aesculus (Horse
chestnut)
Amelanchier (June
berry)
Castanea (Sweet
chestnut)

61

CHAPTER 7

Planting

Planting for the organic garden is basically the same as for conventional gardening. The depth of planting will obviously depend upon the type of plant – a tree needing plenty of depth as opposed to a seed which will only need a few millimetres.

Trees, Shrubs, Roses and Herbaceous Plants

This section includes both fruit and ornamental trees, fruit bushes and ornamental shrubs. All soil should have been cultivated as described in earlier chapters.

Step one Check either with plans of the house or by contacting the local electric, gas and water boards to see if there are any pipes or cables in the chosen site. Once you are satisfied that there are no obstructions, mark where the holes are to be dug. Spacing is all-important; it is vital to know the eventual height and spread of the tree or shrub, and whether its roots will affect the surrounding area, such as pathways and walls. Bad planning at the planting stage can mean wasting years of growth.

Step two Trees will need a deep root run, but care should be taken not to cover the graft mark of those classed as 'bottom worked' (i.e. grafted at the bottom of the tree), *see* Fig 66.

NOTE Most trees are grafted at the bottom (bottom worked), but there are also trees grafted at the top (top worked), such as some of the small weeping varieties.

Fig 66 A graft mark on an apple is shown by the two different colours of wood.

Dig out the hole, placing the soil by the side of the hole. Care should be taken not to smooth the sides of the hole, and pushing a fork into the sides as shown in Fig 67, is a good way of avoiding this problem. Dig down to the desired depth and width – enough to take the root system. Before planting, fork over the bottom of the hole and incorporate well-rotted organic matter (in preference to valuable and fast-disappearing supplies of peat) as shown in Fig 68(a). Place the tree in the hole and spread out the root system as shown in Fig 68(b). Before filling in with the soil, mix in with it a small amount of well-rotted organic matter. Replace the soil, making sure that it is mixed in between the root system. This can be done by lifting the tree slightly and shaking the root. Continue to fill in the hole, at the same time firming with your heel as shown in Fig 68(c).

When you reach the top of the hole there are two ways of finishing off. You can allow a gully either to hold water (which will suit those who live in low rainfall areas), see Fig 69(a), or to drain it away (which will suit those who live in areas of heavy rainfall), see Fig 69(b).

Fig 67   Avoid having smooth sides to the hole by pushing a fork into it.

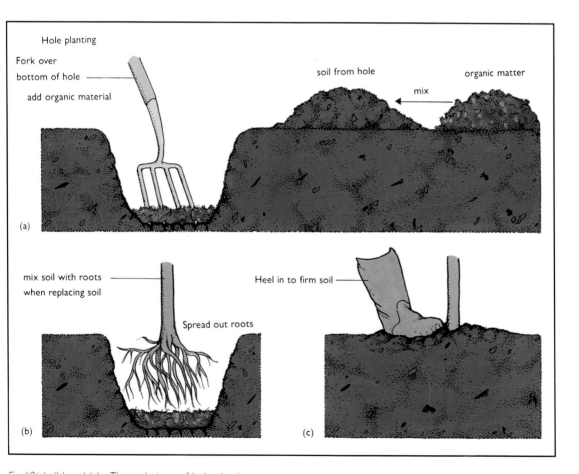

Fig 68(a), (b) and (c)   The technique of hole planting.

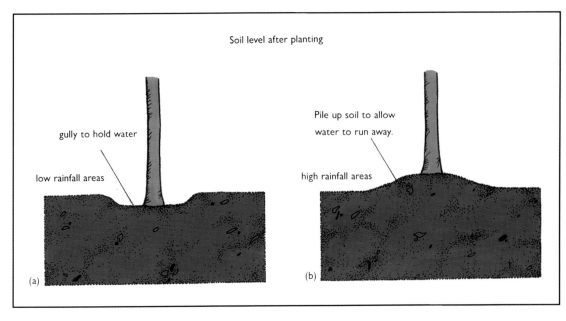

Fig 69(a) and (b) *Two ways of finishing off planting.*

Stakes and ties

The size of the tree and the wind speeds normally reached in your area will govern whether the tree will need a stake or not. A good strong wooden stake should outlast the staking time of the tree (1–2 years generally, but in some cases its complete life). In most cases it is better to use two ties, one approximately a third of the way up from the bottom of the trunk, and the other at the top. Regular checks and adjustments should be made to the tie to stop damage to the trunk.

Seeds and Seedlings

First cultivate the soil as described in previous chapters. After feeding it with a top-dressing such as dried blood, bonemeal and wood ash (if needed), bring the soil to a fine tilth, having levelled it and removed large stones. Mark out the area for sowing. The depth and spacing of seed and rows should be as stated on your seed packet. With a draw hoe (and using a wooden board to walk on if not following the non-dig system) form a drill as shown in Fig 68(a). After planting your seed replace the soil and level by

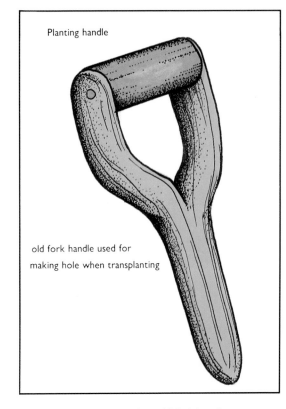

Fig 70 *The top section of an old fork handle will make an ideal soil 'dibber'.*

using both the back and the teeth of a rake (see Fig 68(a), (b), (c)).

Transplanting Seedlings

After cultivating the soil as described, bring it to a fine tilth. Dig small holes to accommodate the root ball of the plants. The holes can be dug with a small hand trowel or hand fork, but remember not to make the sides of the holes too smooth.

After all plantings water should be given, the amount depending upon the weather conditions at the time. Seedlings which need protection from frost can be covered with cloches, and those that need protecting from birds can be covered with nets. Another form of protection is the erection of barriers, for instance in the case of carrots to protect them from carrot fly (see Chapter II). Wind-breaks, which are beneficial to all forms of plant life, are discussed in Chapter 11.

CHAPTER 8

Ponds

Water can play a very important part in an organic garden by attracting insects and therefore helping to bring about a balance between pests and predators. The size of the pond will depend on the amount of room available; where small children are concerned it would be advisable to construct a small pond in the form of a tub and fence it off altogether. If you do decide on a larger pond, take every precaution to ensure the safety of your own and any visiting children.

The larger pond can be divided into five sections:

1) Deep water plants such as lilies.
2) Shallow water, marginal plants.
3) Bog plants for waterlogged areas.
4) Moisture-loving plants for soil around pond.
5) Rock plants and small conifers, again for surrounding area.

Fig 71 A garden pond.

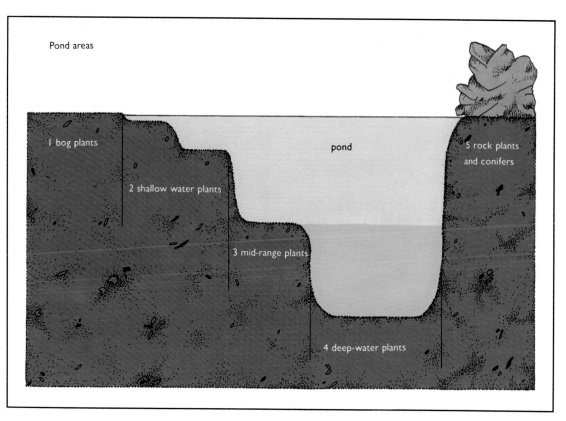

Pond areas

1 bog plants

2 shallow water plants

3 mid-range plants

4 deep-water plants

pond

5 rock plants
and conifers

Fig 72   The different levels for planting aquatic plants.

Building the Pond

Step one   Having decided on the size of the pond, mark out the area in the desired shape and begin the hard work of digging it out. All soil taken from the pond area can be heaped up to make a rock garden, if you like this kind of garden feature.

Step two   A plastic liner or a fibreglass pond may be used. The fibreglass comes in several different colours including one with a gritty, stone texture.

Remove any sharp stones that may be protruding from the sides or the bottom of the hole, then bank up the sides and the bottom with fine sand. This will help to bed in both the liner and the fibreglass pool. If you wish to build a shelf system for plants, blocks placed at different levels as shown in Fig 75 will give a good flat surface for

Fig 73   Soil dug out at the start of making a pond.

67

Fig 74   Suitable fibreglass pools.

Fig 75   By laying blocks as shown, plants can be placed at different depths.

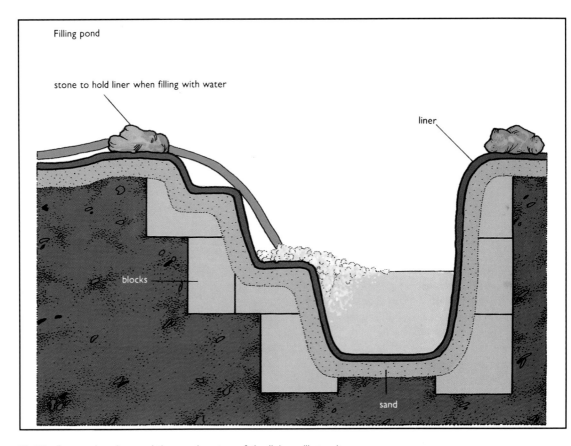

Filling pond

stone to hold liner when filling with water

liner

blocks

sand

Fig 76   Stones placed around the pond on top of the lining will stop it slipping when filling the pond with water.

the plant baskets to stand on. In the case of the fibreglass pool it is just a case of filling in around the sides and then filling with water. The liner must be placed in the hole, with great care being taken not to walk on it or damage it. Several stones or bricks are then placed around the edge to stop it from being pulled in by the weight of the water when filling (*see* Fig 76).

Finding the Balance in the Pond

Problems such as pea green water when the pond is overrun with algae have to be solved without the aid of chemicals. One answer is to grow water plants: if one third or more of the surface area is covered with the foliage of water-lilies and floating plants, the algae will be reduced owing to the lack of light. Another answer is to keep a balance between oxygenating plants, deep-water plants, floating plants and marginal plants; a third solution is the correct balance of fish.

Fig 78   Fish are an added attraction to any pond.

Fig 77   Plant basket for water plants are lined with hessian and then filled with soil to secure the plant in position.

PLANTS FOR PONDS

Insect-eating/Floating Plant:

Name	*Utricularia vulgaris* (Bladderwort)
Water depth	30cm–1 metre
Flower colour	Yellow

Plants which require Deep Water

Nymphaea (Water lily)

Name	*N. alba*
Water depth	60–120cm
Flower spread	10–15cm
Flower colour	White with yellow stamens

N. odorata – Various varieties

Name	*N. o. Minor*
Water depth	30–40cm
Flower spread	5–8cm
Flower colour	White

Fig 79   A water lily.

Name	N. o. Sulphurea
Water depth	23–30cm
Flower spread	8cm
Flower colour	Primrose-yellow

Name	N. o. Turicensis
Water depth	30cm
Flower spread	7–10cm
Flower colour	Pale pink (scented)

Name	Froebelii
Water depth	30–80cm
Flower spread	10cm
Flower colour	Deep red (slightly scented)

N. laydekeri

Name	N. l. Fulgens
Water depth	20–60cm
Flower spread	10cm
Flower colour	Bright red-pink with orange-red stamens

Name	N. l Purpurata
Water depth	20–60cm

Flower spread	8–10cm
Flower colour	Deep pink – rose crimson

N. marliacea

Name	N. m. Albida
Water depth	45cm–1 metre
Flower spread	10–15cm
Flower colour	White

Name	Rose Arey
Water depth	30–45cm
Flower spread	10–15cm
Flower colour	Deep pink with yellow stamens

Name	William Falconer
Water depth	30–45cm
Flower spread	10–15cm
Flower colour	Beetroot red

Name	N. capensis
Water depth	20–40cm
Flower spread	10–12cm
Flower colour	Light blue

Name	N. stellata
Water depth	20–40cm
Flower spread	10–15cm
Flower colour	Lavender blue with golden stamens (heavily scented)

Name	Missouri
Water depth	20–40cm
Flower spread	15–30cm
Flower colour	White with yellow stamens

Name	Mrs G. C. Hitchcock
Water depth	20–40cm
Flower spread	15–30cm
Flower colour	Deep pink changing to white at centre with deep pink stamens

Oxygenating plants

Name	Anacharis canadensis (Candian pond weed)
Water depth	30cm–1 metre

Fig 80   An oxygenating plant.

Fig 81   A water hyacinth.

Foliage colour   Dark green

Name   *Hottonia palustris* (Water violet)
Water depth   30cm–1 metre
Flower spread   Flowers will develop on stems 20–30cm
Flower colour   Pale lilac
Foliage colour   Pale green

Name   *Lagarosiphon major* (Curled anacharis)
Water depth   30cm–1 metre
Flower colour   Dark green

Name   *Myriophyllum* (Milfoil)
Water depth   30cm–1 metre
Flower colour   Green-red

Name   *Ranunculus aquatilis* (Water buttercup or water crowfoot)
Water depth   30cm–1 metre
Flower colour   White

Floating Plants

Name   *Azolla caroliniana* (Fairy moss)
Water depth   30cm–1 metre
Foliage colour   Light green, sometimes tinged red

Name   *Hydrocharis morsus-ranae* (Frogbit)
Water depth   30cm–1 metre
Flower colour   White

Name   *Trapa natans* (Water chestnut)
Water depth   30cm–1 metre
Flower colour   White

Plants for Shallow Water

Name   *Acorus* (Sweet flag)
Water depth   10cm soil and 8cm water
Height   60–65cm
Foliage colour   Green leaves edged in creamy white

Name   *Butomus umbellatus* (Flowering rush)
Water depth   Up to 9cm

71

Height	45cm–1 metre
Foliage colour	Deep green
Flower colour	Pink

Name	*Calla palustris* (Bog arum)
Water depth	10cm soil and 8cm water
Height	15cm
Foliage colour	Dark green
Flower colour	White

Iris laevigata (Water iris)

Name	*I. l. alba*
Water depth	10cm soil and 8cm water
Flower colour	White

Name	*I. l. pseudacorus*
Water depth	10cm soil and 8cm water
Height	1–1.5m
Flower colour	Golden yellow

Name	*Myosotis palustris* (Mermaid)
Water depth	10cm soil and 8cm water
Height	20–25cm
Flower colour	China blue with yellow centre

Name	*Pontederia cordata* (Pickerel)
Water depth	10cm soil and 8cm water
Height	45–60cm
Flower colour	Blue with golden centre

Name	*Scirpus* (True bulrush)
Water depth	10cm soil and 8cm water
Height	120cm
Stem colour	White with green vertical stripes

Moisture-Loving Plants

Name	*Astilbe*
Height	45–120cm
Flower colour	Red, pink or white

Name	*Hosta glauca* (Plantain lily)
Height	60–65cm
Foliage colour	Grey-blue, ribbed
Leaf spread	30–40cm

Iris

Name	*I. kaempferi*
Height	60–65cm
Flower colour	Purple, dark to light blue or white, often veined with another colour
Flower spread	10–20cm

Name	*I. forrestii*
Height	60cm
Flower spread	6cm
Flower colour	Pale yellow

Name	*Peltiphyllum peltatum* (Umbrella plant)
Height	45cm
Flower colour	Pink

Primula (Primrose)

Name	*P. aurantiaca*
Height	30cm
Flower colour	Yellow-orange

Name	*P. beesiana*
Height	60cm
Flower colour	Lilac-purple with yellow eye

Name	*P. florindae*
Height	Up to 2m
Flower colour	Generally pale yellow, but can also be from light orange to deep red

Name	*Onoclea sensibilis* (Sensitive fern)
Height	30–60cm
Foliage colour	Pale green
Pests and diseases	Generally trouble free; however, susceptible to sharp frost

Name	*Dryopteris cristata* (Crested buckler fern)
Height	60cm
Foliage colour	Pale green

CHAPTER 9

Fruit

A careful study of varieties that are resistant or less susceptible to pest and diseases, or rootstocks that are immune to some forms of disease, will help to avoid the need for chemical insecticides and fungicides. In fact, research has produced rootstocks that will do better in poor soils, and these will therefore stand up better to natural elements when grown organically without the aid of chemical feeds. Certain rootstocks will also produce smaller trees, ideally suited to the smaller garden. A knowledge of flowering times is important, both to ensure pollination and to avoid frost damage; pruning plays a signifi-cant part in the health of trees and bushes, allowing light and air to get to the centre of the plant, thus helping to fight diseases.

Tree Shapes

The average garden today is far too small to grow several large fruit trees, but it is now possible to grow them on dwarf rootstocks. They may be grown in several different shapes: as cordons, espaliers, dwarf pyramids or small bush trees.

Fig 82   Two basic tree shapes. (a) Cordon.

(b) Fan.

Fig 83(a) Free-standing fruit cage.

Fruit Cage

If you have the room, a fruit cage can be very useful in helping to control attacks from birds. The cage will also act as a windbreak, offer protection from frost and give some shelter from heavy rain and hail stones, as well as providing some shading during periods of very hot sunny weather.

Wall fruit cage Small fruit cages such as the one shown in Fig 83(b) can be erected to stop birds from attacking trees which are grown against a wall.

Soil

The apple, pear, plum and cherry are well suited to deep cultivation with organic matter and to the use of raised beds to provide a deeper root run (*see* Chapter 4, page 38). Some cherries prefer grassed areas to a cultivated topsoil.

Planting

It is very important that the union – the area where the rootstock and the scion or bud join – is not buried in the soil, otherwise the top section (scion) may take root, and larger trees without fruit will grow.

Spacing The space between each tree will depend upon the type of rootstock – dwarf or vigorous – and the style of tree, such as bush, cordon, etc. In addition, it is only common sense to find out the eventual height and spread of the tree before planting, as over-crowding can produce a multitude of problems.

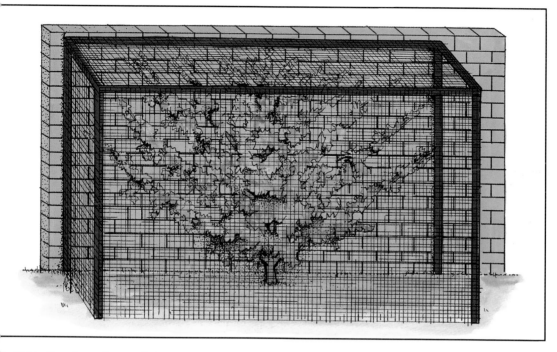

Fig 83(b)   Cage for wall-grown fruit.

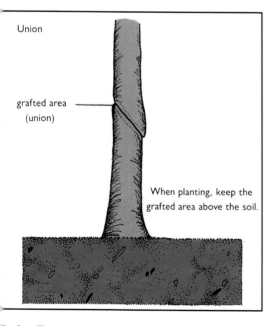

Union

grafted area
(union)

When planting, keep the
grafted area above the soil.

Fig 84   The graft mark or 'union' of a fruit
tree.

PRUNING

Pruning for Health

It is no good correcting the soil, providing a
drainage system, and spending hours studying
rootstocks, varieties and pest life cycles, if you
leave stumps to rot and branches to rub against
each other, stopping light and air from circulating
around the plant. The most important points to
consider when starting your pruning are dead,
damaged and diseased wood, followed by crossing branches. Once the three Ds and crossing
branches have been taken out, very little pruning
is needed. There are other forms of pruning,
such as spur and renewal pruning, and there is a
form of cosmetic pruning which allows light and
air to reach the centre of the plant as well as the
fruit.

75

Fig 85 *All dead sections should be removed.*

The Three Ds

Dead wood This is an excellent breeding ground for diseases, and it does not take very long for insects to start burrowing into the soft, decaying wood, building nests and laying eggs for future generations. Very soon apparently harmless sections of dead wood become a complete disaster area for the tree. The diseases and pests are not content with colonising the dead area, but will start to move into other sections of the tree. In some cases they can also be transported by the wind or on the feathers of birds and in the fur of animals to other plants growing close by. Therefore, cut out all dead sections as soon as possible, and never leave stumps which will die back and cause such areas (*see* Fig 88(d)).

Damaged wood Although a branch may still show healthy signs of life, if it is damaged then sooner or later some form of disease will enter the tree through this section. Pruning to prevent is therefore better than pruning to cure.

Diseased wood Diseases such as canker and coral spot should be removed by pruning as soon as discovered (*see* Chapter 11).

Crossing Branches

Branches which are allowed to grow into one another will rub during strong winds, damaging themselves and other branches, which in turn will allow diseases to enter the tree. All crossing branches should be removed during annual pruning.

Hygiene note Never leave old pruning wood lying about, and never compost or burn diseased wood and then recycle it. Always keep piles of wood ready for burning, and canes, etc, away from growing areas, to avoid the danger of pests breeding and over-wintering. Canes make especially good breeding grounds: their hollow stems offer insects warmth and protection during the winter months.

Fig 86 *Old wood makes an ideal breeding ground for pests and diseases.*

Pruning Cuts

Cutting back to the correct position is a very important factor when growing organically, and not only cutting back to the right point, but also at the correct angle, which allows water to run away from the wound or bud.

Bud Shapes

On some fruits such as apples, pears and plums, it is important to know the difference between a leaf bud and a flowering bud. Some people may use the term 'fruiting bud', but when the tree has not been pollinated for one reason or another, the tree can flower without producing fruit, and it would therefore be better to call it a flowering rather than a fruiting bud.

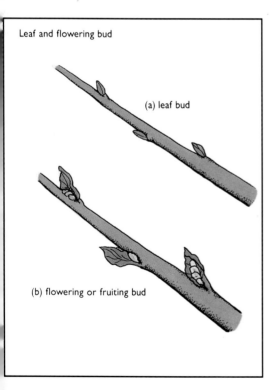

Leaf and flowering bud

(a) leaf bud

(b) flowering or fruiting bud

Fig 87   The leaf bud tends to be flat against the wood (a). Flowering buds are cigar-shaped (b).

Pruning for Spurs

The term 'spur' is used for small groups of flowering buds growing from sub-laterals of a side (lateral) branch. The spurs found on fruit trees are encouraged through pruning and should produce an abundance of flowering buds which, if pollinated when open, will produce a good crop of fruit. The spur starts forming on the second year's wood, and the first year's growth is cut back in November to 2 or 3 buds to encourage lateral growth. After this, pruning takes place twice a year, in the late autumn (November through to February, but I prefer November if possible), and following the June drop, when the fruitlets are starting to form between July and September. Pruning during the summer will not only help to form the spur, it will also allow light and air to reach the developing fruit.

Spur Thinning

After several years you will find that the spur becomes too crowded and the fruit will compete for space, light and air. This is when you should thin the spur as shown in Fig 89.

Thinning Fruit

The term 'June drop' means exactly that. Around this time a certain amount of the young forming fruit will fall from the tree. This is a quite natural process, with the tree trying to thin its own crop. However, where fruit still remains overcrowded, thinning has to take place. The amount of fruit left in one section of the spur can range from 1–3 but common sense should rule, and if two or more fruits are touching, one or more of them should be removed with sharp secateurs or specially designed long-handled scissors.

Renewal Pruning

To gain the maximum crop, combine spur pruning on the older section of the tree and renewal

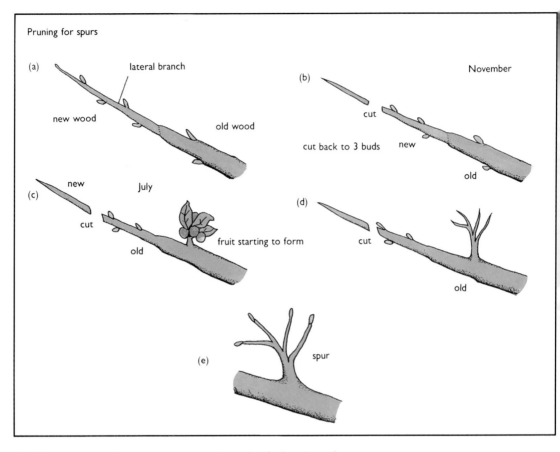

Fig 88(a)   By pruning the growing tips, lateral branches further down the
tree will be encouraged to grow.
(b) and (c)   Large cigar-shaped buds are those which produce
flowers and these in turn produce fruit when pollinated.
(d)   Avoid leaving stumps.
(e)   Spurs are produced on old wood.

pruning on the new growth section. This is similar to spur pruning, but the fruit is produced on a long branch spur rather than a short stumpy group spur, and the renewal method replaces the complete branch in the third year. This encourages healthy new growth, but at the same time keeps the tree within its growing boundaries.

Care should be taken when pruning these trees which produce fruit at the end of their branches — known as 'Tip Bearers'. The apple tree 'Bramley's Seedling' is a tip bearer, although fruit is also produced on spurs on older sections of the tree. This would be a case for renewal pruning to avoid removing fruiting branches.

Other Pruning

See Pruning plums and damsons, page 90.

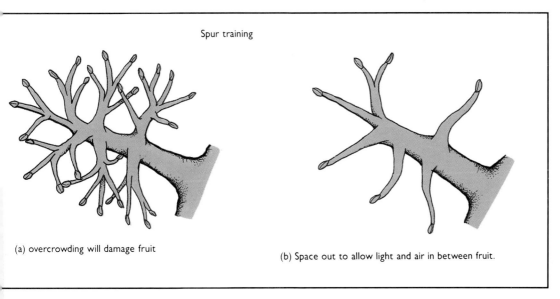

Spur training

(a) overcrowding will damage fruit

(b) Space out to allow light and air in between fruit.

Fig 89   Spur training – spurs will need thinning to avoid fruit from becoming overcrowded.

Fig 90   Long-handled scissors are ideal for fruit pruning and avoid damaging the outer branches.

APPLES

Growing apples organically is basically the same as growing apples in the usual way, but the conditions for growing organically should be as perfect as possible because the trees will need more strength and vigour than their counterparts grown non-organically which have the advantage of chemical feeds, insecticides and fungicides. The organic grower has to create a natural balance and combine a study of pest and disease life cycles and resistant rootstocks. It would be misleading to suggest that growing organically will produce perfectly healthy food; indeed, you will need to take cosmetic measures such as removing scab by pruning, unless scab-resistant trees such as 'Egremont Russet' are planted. Always follow the practice of cutting into the fruit before eating or cooking to check for pest. To grow apples with any success it would be advisable to wait until you have a balanced soil with good drainage, especially if you wish to grow such varieties as 'Cox's Orange Pippin'. Without balanced soil, and even more importantly, with-

79

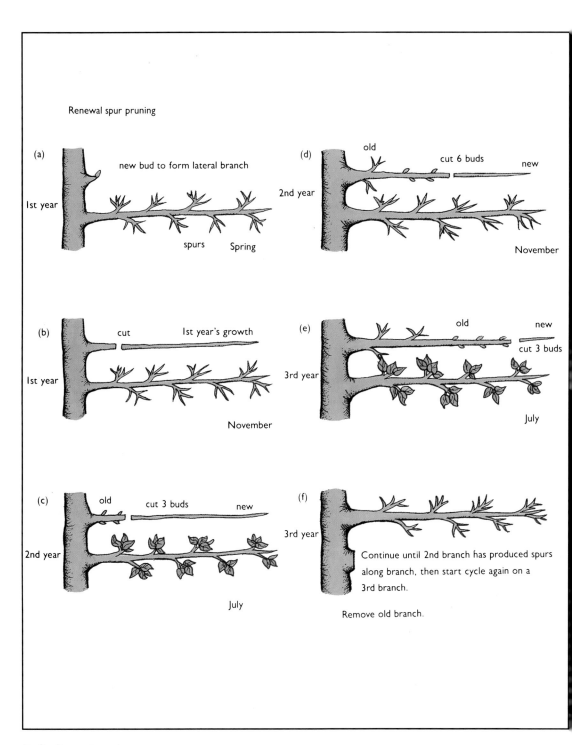

Renewal spur pruning

(a) 1st year
new bud to form lateral branch
spurs   Spring

(d) 2nd year
old   cut 6 buds   new
November

(b) 1st year
cut   1st year's growth
November

(e) 3rd year
old   new
cut 3 buds
July

(c) 2nd year
old   cut 3 buds   new
July

(f) 3rd year
Continue until 2nd branch has produced spurs along branch, then start cycle again on a 3rd branch.

Remove old branch.

Fig 91   Renewal pruning.

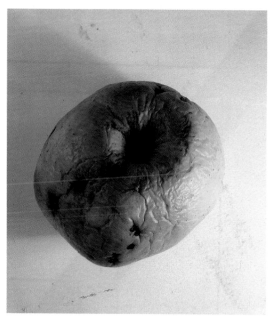

Fig 92(a) and (b) When growing organic fruit, for cosmetic reasons you may have to cut away the unsightly parts before eating. Always cut the fruit in half first to check for insects.

out drainage, this variety will soon be prey to diseases such as apple canker. However, you will find that most apples, of the cooking and eating kind, will crop far better when planted in a soil which allows for a deep root run, between 2–4 metres. One way of overcoming the problem of depth is the raised bed system, (*see* page 38).

Soil *See* Chapter 4.

Pests and diseases *See* Chapter 11.

Pollination and Time of Flowering

Flowering times must be taken into consideration when purchasing your tree, whether it is an apple, pear, plum or cherry, for two reasons: the pollination factor, and weather conditions.

Pollination factor Apples and pears, some plums and most cherries will not produce a proper crop unless they are cross-pollinated with another compatible variety. There are seven groups in the apple section, each containing trees which flower at the same time, and therefore it is important that you purchase trees from the same group or from groups which overlap, rather than one tree from the first group and one from the last. If this rule is not followed then pollination cannot take place, because the first tree has lost its blossom before the second has started to flower. Whether a tree is biennial or triploid will also affect pollination success (*see* page 82).

Weather conditions factor If you happen to live in an area prone to late frost, it is important that you choose apples which are late flowering, such as those from Group 3 or 4, thereby helping to avoid possible frost damage to the flowers, which endangers the chance of flowers being pollinated and producing fruit.

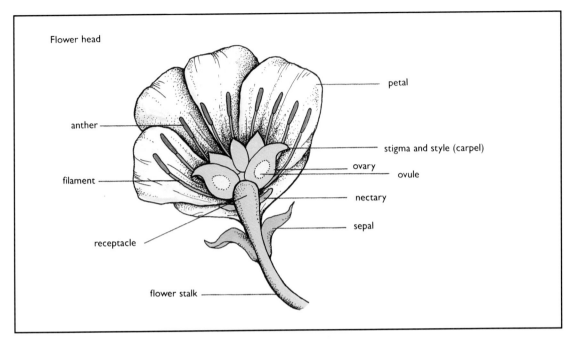

Fig 93   The important sections of a flower.

Apple Groups

To mention all the apple varieties would be impossible here, therefore I have listed just a few of the better known ones, and problems such as biennial and triploid trees.

Biennial Trees

These are fruit trees which can miss a flowering period one year, but flower the next. Care should be taken when choosing such a tree not to use it as a pollinator for other trees. To ensure pollination takes place, two other non-biennial trees from the same group or overlapping groups should be planted with it. The list below contains only a few of the biennial trees available, and it would be advisable to seek further advice from your local nursery.

Biennial Apple Tree Groups

Group 1   'Mank's Codlin'

Group 2   'Adam's Pearmain'
'Ben's Red'
'Christmas Pearmain'

Group 3   'Allington Pippin'
'Fortune'
'Red Victoria'

Group 4   'Gladstone'
'Monarch'
'Laxton's Superb'

Group 5   'Coronation'
'Northern Spy'
'Woolbrook Pippin'

Triploid Trees

Most apple trees are termed 'diploid' that is, they contain the usual number of chromosomes, half derived from the male parent and half from the female. However, there are a few which are termed 'triploid', that is, they have 1½ times the normal number of chromosomes in the nucleus of any cell. Poor pollination will result from two triploid trees grown together; it is far better if a triploid tree is planted with two diploid ones. The following 3 groups are triploids, but further advice should be sought when purchasing your tree.

Group 1 'Gravenstein'

Group 2 'Ribston Pippin'
'Washington'

Group 3 'Bramley's Seedling'
'Crispin'

General Groups

The following groups are all diploid trees, but space dictates that the list is limited to a few well-known trees.

Group 1 This is the early flowering group, and I would advise you to choose a later flowering tree if possible, unless a sheltered position is available.
'Lord Suffield'
'Red Astrachan'

Group 2 Another early flowering group; a sheltered position is advisable to protect from frost.

'Beauty of Bath'	'Lord Lambourne'
'Egremont Russet'	'Merton Charm'
'Golden Spire'	'Norfolk Beauty'
'Idared'	'St Edmund's
'Laxton's Early	Pippin'
Crimson'	

Group 3 This is the largest group and probably the best group to start from to avoid frost damage.

'Charles Ross'	'Discovery'
'Chivers Delight'	'Granny Smith'
'Cox's Orange	'Greensleeves'
Pippin'	'Grenadier'

'James Grieve'	'Spartan'
'Jonathan'	'Sunset'
'Malling Kent'	'Tydeman's Early
'Merton Russet'	Worcester'
'Merton Worcester'	'Worcester Pearmain'

Group 4 Later flowering than Group 3, again a good group to start with.

'Delicious'	'Laxton's Pearmain'
'Ellison's Orange'	'Lord Derby'
'Golden Delicious'	'Mannington's
'Golden Noble'	Pearmain'
'Lane's Prince	'Pixie'
Albert'	

Group 5
'Merton Beauty'
'Newton Wonder'
'Royal Jubilee'

Group 6
'Bess Pool'
'Edward VII'
'Laxton's Royalty'

Group 7 'Crawley Beauty'. (If conditions allow, it will set fruit without cross-pollination.)

Rootstocks

Selected rootstock produced through many years of research at East Malling in Kent will help in organic fruit-growing for three reasons. The first is that it can give you more control over size and vigour, such as the dwarf rootstock M.IX, which is suitable for small areas and cordon or dwarf pyramid growing. The second reason is that, if you are unable to produce a balanced fertile soil, selected rootstocks such as M.I.M.XII and M.XVI can be used to counteract the lack of vigour in your soil. The third reason is that some rootstocks have been developed to help fight pests and diseases (*see* Rootstock list, overleaf).

You may find that rootstocks will change as new ones are found and the older forms are dis-

Fig 94 The rootstock is the part with light brown wood, while the dark part is the scion or section that has been grafted on to the root stock.

carded. However, I have listed both some of the older ones and some newer forms. Keep abreast of developments by consulting your local nursery or by writing to the Ministry of Agriculture for up-to-date information each year.

Rootstock List

M.IX	Very dwarf rootstock, needs a more fertile soil than the vigorous rootstocks.
M.7	Semi-dwarf.
M.9	Dwarf, ideal for small gardens.
M.26	More vigorous than M.IX.
M.VII	Semi-dwarf, good early cropper.
M.II	Vigorous and will increase in vigour as it becomes older, very good cropper and ideal for poor soils (*see also* MM.109 and MM.111).
M.I	Vigorous, but I prefer M.II.
M.XII	More vigorous than M.II and M.I, but takes a long time to come into bearing.

M.XVI Again, a very vigorous rootstock, needs plenty of room. Trees on this rootstock can be fairly large.

Rootstocks/Malling – Merton Series

This is a series of rootstocks which have been crossed with the East Malling stocks, and the variety 'Northern Spy', which is known to be immune from attacks by woolly aphids, is a good one for an organic programme.

MM.104	Medium vigour.
MM.106	Semi-dwarfing stock.
MM.109	Vigorous, use instead of M.II.
MM.111	Vigorous, use instead of M.II.

Apples for Cooking

'Bramley's Seedling'	Cooker, October – March; large fruit, which can be damaged by frost.
'Crispin'	Cooker and dessert, December – February.
'Golden Noble'	Cooker, September – January.
'Grenadier'	Cooker, sometimes used as a dessert, early August and September, scab resistant.
'Newton Wonder'	Cooker and dessert, November – March, large fruits.
'Peasgood's Nonsuch'	Cooker and dessert, October – November.

Apples for Freezing

'Bramley's Seedling'

Fig 95   A Bramley is an excellent cooking apple.

Fig 96   The Cox's apple seems a popular choice for the first-time grower. Perhaps this is because its name is easy to remember?

Apples for Eating

'Cox's Orange Pippin'	Dessert, November – January. Poor disease resistance, can be damaged by frost.
'Egremont Russet'	Dessert, October – December, scab resistant.
'Ellison's Orange'	Dessert, September and October.
'George Cave'	Dessert, mid – late August.
'James Grieve'	Dessert, good tree for small areas, September, easily bruised. Can resist frosts, but prone to diseases.
'Laxton's Fortune'	Dessert, September and October, frost resistant.
'Lord Lambourne'	Dessert, October and November. Excellent alternative to 'Cox's Orange Pippin' if soil unsuitable with poor drainage.
'Merton Russet'	Dessert, December – February, small fruits.
'Merton Worcester'	Dessert, September and October.
'Orleans Reinette'	Dessert, January and February, prone to canker.
'St Edmund's Pippin'	Dessert, September and October, small apples.
'Sturmer Pippin'	Dessert, December – March, ideally requires warm area (south facing) to achieve a good crop.
'Sunset'	Dessert, October – December, another good alternative to Cox's Orange Pippin if soil unsuitable due to drainage problems.

'Tydeman's Early'	Dessert, late August, early September.
'Worcester Pearmain'	Dessert, August – September, prone to scab.

PEARS

Pears are grown in basically the same way as apples, and a balanced soil with a deep root run is ideal, but remember that growing organically will entail constant checks on the tree for pest and disease. Pruning will help to control or avoid diseases to a certain extent, as described earlier (see page 75).

Soil *See* Chapter 4.

Pests and diseases *See* Chapter 11.

Flowering times There are four groups in the pear section which relate to flowering times. As with apples, there are triploid trees, so if you choose a variety of pear that is triploid, make sure you plant two different varieties from the same group or overlap from the group next to it to ensure pollination.

Triploid Pears

Group 1 'Maréchal de la Cour'

Group 2 'Beurré Alexander Lucas'
'Vicar of Winkfield'

Group 3 'Doyenné Boussoch'
'Merton Pride'

Group 4 'Catillac'
'Pitmaston Duchess'

Ineffective Pollinators

There are a few other pears which, if planted with another tree, will not act as a pollinator, and it is therefore advisable to plant three trees of different varieties rather than two. The ineffective pollinators are:
'Marguerite Marillat'
'Beurré Bedford'
'Bristol Cross'
Listed below are a few well-known diploid pears. There is a wide range in this section – too many to list here – therefore seek further advice when purchasing from your local nursery.

Diploid Pears

Group 1 Brockworth Park'

Group 2

'Beurré d'Anjou'	'Louise Bonne of
'Beurré Giffard'	Jersey'
'Doyenné d'Eté'	'Princess'
	'Packham's Triumph'

Group 3

'Beurré Dumont'	'Laxton's Early
'Beurré Hardy'	Market'
'Conference'	'Laxton's Progress'
'Dr Jules Guyot'	'Laxton's
'Fertility'	Satisfaction'
'Joséphine de	'Williams' Bon
Malines'	Chrétien'

Group 4

'Doyenné du	'Onward'
Comice'	'Winter Nelis'
'Laxton's Formost'	
'Laxton's Victor'	

Rootstock

The rootstock for the pear tree is quince, and budding is used instead of grafting. The problem that arises from the quince stock is that only certain varieties are compatible. One such variety is 'Beurré Hardy' and this variety can be used as our first stage. The reason it is called the first stage is because you can not only allow the quince rootstock and the budded 'Beurré

Hardy' to grow into a full-size tree, but you can also, after a growing season, bud on to 'Beurré Hardy' other varieties that are not compatible with the quince rootstock. This practice is termed 'double-working'.

Rootstock List

Malling Quince A   Dwarfing rootstock
Malling Quince B   Semi-vigorous

When choosing your varieties, look for those which have the advantage of disease resistance: 'Williams' Bon Chrétien', for instance, is susceptible to pear scab whereas 'Conference' is not.

Listed below are varieties of cooking and eating pears together with suitable pollinators.

Pears for Cooking

'Pitmaston Duchess'   Cooker, pollinated by 'Conference'.

Pears for Freezing

'Doyenné du Comice'   Dessert, pollinated by 'Conference', or 'Williams' Bon Chrétien' (prone to scab), also good for eating.

'Williams' Bon Chrétien   Dessert, prone to scab, pollinated by 'Conference' and 'Joséphine de Malines'.

Pears for Eating

'Conference'   Dessert, almost immune to scab, pollinated by 'Joséphine de Malines' or 'Williams' Bon

Chrétien' (prone to scab).

'Dr Jules Guyot'   Dessert, pollinated by 'Doyenné du Comice', 'Conference' and 'Fertility' (prone to scab).

'Fertility'   Dessert, susceptible to scab, pollinated by 'Dr Jules Guyot', 'Doyenné du Comice' or 'Winter Nelis'.

'Joséphine de Malines'   Dessert, pollinated by 'Conference', 'Louise Bonne of Jersey' and 'Williams' Bon Chrétien' (prone to scab).

'Louise Bonne of Jersey'   Dessert, pollinated by 'Joséphine de Malines'.

'Packham's Triumph'   Dessert, pollinated by 'Joséphine de Malines', 'Williams' Bon Chrétien' (prone to scab).

'Winter Nellis'   Dessert, pollinated by 'Doyenné du Comice'.

PLUMS AND GAGES

Plums and gages need the same kind of soil and planting conditions as apples and pears. Care should be taken with the pruning, (see , page 90). As with most plants, some are more susceptible than others to attacks from diseases and bacterial infections, and the old favourite 'Victoria', along with others such as 'Czar', tend to be more vulnerable. However, this does not mean that you should not plant them; be aware of the problems of individual plants.

Soil *See* Chapter 4.

Pests and diseases *See* Chapter 11.

Rootstocks

The rootstock can play an important part in controlling the growth rate and vigour of the tree. Some rootstocks will help in the fight against such diseases as silver leaf. The common plum rootstock, for instance, will offer some defence against the disease. The rootstock for the plum and gage is produced by layering, and the most common ones are listed below.

Common plum	Dwarfing rootstock, good for small gardens.
'Pixy'	Dwarfing rootstock, ideal for small and compact trees.
'St Julien A'	Again, a semi-dwarfing rootstock ideal for small gardens and fruit cage growing.
'Brampton'	Vigorous, suitable for the larger garden, or for less than ideal soils.
'Myrobalan B'	More vigorous than 'Brampton' and once again suitable for the larger garden or poor soils.

Five groups from early to late make up the flowering times of the plum, but always check with your local nursery for new varieties. *See also* Self-compatible Plums section.

Group 1 'Jefferson'

Group 2 'Coe's Golden Drop'
'Denniston's Superb'

Group 3 'Czar'
'Golden Transparent'
'Laxton's Gage'
'Victoria'

Group 4 'Kirke's'
'Cambridge Gage'
'Early Transparent Gage'

Group 5 'Kentish Bush'
'Laxton's Blue Tit (both trees are self-compatible)

Self-compatible Plums

Suitable for growing on their own.

'Czar'	*See* below, Plums for Cooking.
'Denniston's Superb'	Dessert, mid-August, good variety for small garden and fruit cage.
'Early Transparent Gage'	Dessert, mid-August.
'Golden Transparent'	Dessert, large plum.
'Laxton's Gage'	Dessert, August, large, free-cropping.
'Victoria'	Dessert, late August, prone to silver leaf disease (use common plum rootstock).

Plums for Cooking

'Czar' Cooker, early August, prone to silver leaf disease (use common plum rootstock).

Plums for Eating

'Cambridge Gage'	Dessert, mid to late August, pollinators are 'Czar', 'Oullin's Golden Gage', 'Golden Transport', and 'Laxton's Gage'.

'Coe's Golden Drop' Dessert, late September – early October, needs pollinator such as 'Early Transparent Gage' or 'Denniston's Superb'. Requires sheltered area (or fruit cage).

'Jefferson' Dessert, early September, needs pollinator such as 'Early Transparent Gage' or 'Denniston's Superb'.

'Kirke's' Dessert, mid September, needs pollinator such as 'Golden Transparent', 'Czar' and 'Laxton's Gage'. Plant on south-facing aspect.

DAMSONS

Prepare the same soil conditions as recommended for apples, pears and plums.

Damsons for Cooking

'Farleigh Damson' Cooker, mid September, pollinate with 'Czar', 'Golden Transparent' and 'Cambridge Gage'.

Tree shapes

(a) before pruning

(b) after pruning

Fig 97 Pruning a fruit tree.

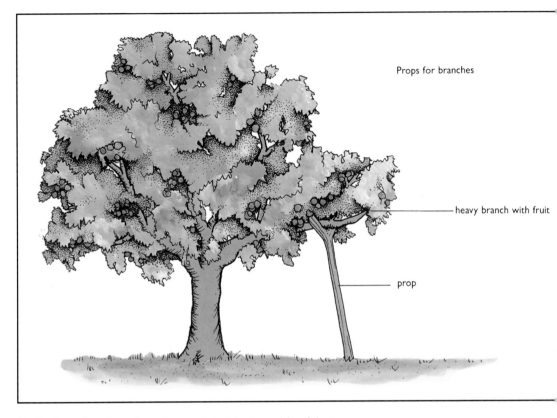

Props for branches

heavy branch with fruit

prop

Fig 98 Some branches will need supports to take the weight of the tree.

Damsons for Eating

'Merryweather' Dessert, late August and
September, self-fertile.

Pruning Plums and Damsons

To cover all the pruning techniques here is impossible, but cutting back to the correct points
(*see* page 77) and pruning at the right time will
help to control diseases such as silver leaf, which
enters through wounds made when pruning. I
prefer summer pruning – between June and
August – which has been found to be more suc-
cessful than winter pruning for plums and damsons. Purchase a tree which already has the basic
shape you require, and avoid allowing it to produce very large branches which will leave large
wounds if pruned. Avoid, too, crossing branches
which will rub and cause open wounds. Some
trees may produce heavy crops; if this is the case
then some form of prop to support the branch
and prevent it breaking is necessary. Cover such
as the fruit cage will stop birds from inflicting
open wounds and damaging fruit.

CHERRIES

There are two kinds of cherry, the sweet and the
acid. Both like a balanced soil with plenty of
depth, but the sweet cherry dislikes cultivation
around the surface area of its root system, which
may in fact cause gumming up or, to give it it

orrect term, gummosis. It prefers a non-ultivated grass area around its roots. Both sweet nd sour cherries should be grown in fruit cages r netted if possible.

oil Both forms of cherry will benefit from the oil cultivation recommended in Chapter 4.

ests and Diseases *See* Chapter 11.

weet Cherry

he sweet cherry is not a tree for the small arden, and it also grows better in groups in a rassy area (sweet cherries will not set fruit nless pollinated by other cherries).

cid Cherries/Duke Cherries/Sour herries

1ainly used for cooking, these can be grown gainst a wall and the soil surface around the root ystem can be cultivated. They can also be grown s a single tree or bush. 'Morello', which is self-ompatible, is particularly suitable.

lowering times

here are five groups in the cherry section; some f them are self-compatible and will set fruit by hemselves, others have part self-compatibility, ut may produce a poor crop, and there are hose which need several trees to pollinate each ther. Rather than try to list all these groups, I ave confined myself to the most popular arieties.

weet Cherries

'Early Rivers'	Good flavour, late June, plant with 'Merton Favourite' for pollination.
'Merton Favourite'	Good flavour, July, plant with 'Early Rivers' for pollination.

Acid Cherries

'Morello'	Self-compatible, August, ideal for planting against a wall.

Rootstocks

The careful choice of rootstock will help in the fight against a pest or a disease. 'Malling F12/1' is a good one, being resistant to bacterial canker. Research is going on into other rootstocks to produce a small tree, and advice should be sought from your local nursery.

Grassing Down for Sweet Cherries

Before planting, bring your soil as close as possible to the balanced ideal recommended in previous chapters. Drainage is of the utmost importance, and raised beds should be used if necessary to provide a deep root run. Plant your tree as described in Chapter 7, working in well-rotted compost below the root and also mixing it in with the soil used to fill in the hole. This will act as a soil conditioner rather than wasting valuable peat. Once you have planted the tree, cultivate the surface of the soil and bring it to a fine tilth. Good results have been produced from sowing perennial ryegrass because it is hard wearing; also, allow clover to take hold as its nitrogen content is beneficial. The grass should be maintained using either a push or electric mower, fitted with a box for collecting the cuttings.

OTHER FORMS OF FRUIT

To cover every form of fruit would take not one but several books; my aim, therefore, is to give a few examples of varieties, but to put most emphasis on the importance of drainage, soil, position and choice of variety in order to suit the growing conditions and pest and disease factors.

Blackberries/Hybrid Berries

This section includes such hybrids as:

Loganberry   A cross between a blackberry and a raspberry.

Boysenberry   A cross between a blackberry, a raspberry and a loganberry.

Soil   Need a well-balanced, cultivated soil with good drainage, but with moisture retention. The blackberry will benefit from a deep root run through cultivation or a raised bed system.

Mulching   Well-rotted straw compost containing f.y.m. should be used as a top-dressing, which will not only benefit the plant, but will also help with weed control and moisture retention.

Planting *See* Chapter 7.

Pests and Diseases *See* Chapter 11.

Fig 99 *Blackberries are very easy to grow and are ideal for freezing.*

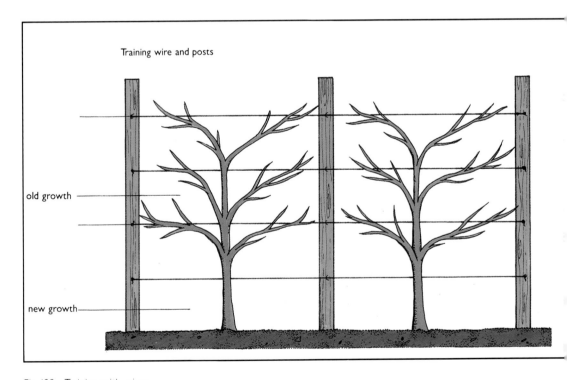

Training wire and posts

old growth

new growth

Fig 100 *Training with wires.*

Pruning After planting, cut the plants down to within 23cm of the ground (some may have already been cut when purchased). Tie the new growth to training wires, which should be 30–35cm apart, as shown in Fig 100. This will allow light and air to the centre of the plant, helping to stop the build-up of fungus diseases.

The fruit is produced on the older wood (A), therefore it is important to keep the new (current year's) growth (B) separated from the older growth when training. Cut out the older growth after fruiting and then move the new growth to replace it. This will allow space for further new growth (C) to be tied in and trained thus, completing a continuous chain of pruning.

Blackberry Varieties

'Bedford Giant'	July
'Himalaya Giant'	September and October
'John Innes'	August and September, sweet fruit.
'Merton Early'	August and September.
'Oregon Thornless'	August and September.

Raspberries

It is always important to purchase good clean plants free from disease. One way of ensuring this is to purchase only those which have a Ministry of Agriculture certificate, and usually all good garden centres will only sell certificated stock.

Soil The raspberry is well suited to organic conditions as it likes plenty of organic matter and a deep cultivated soil.

Planting Plant in rows with each cane 45–48cm apart. See also Chapter 7.

Pests and Diseases See Chapter 11.

The fruiting time can be either summer or autumn. Autumn-fruiting raspberries tend to produce a smaller crop than the summer-fruiting ones; however, by choosing the right varieties you can have a succession of fruit over several months.

Pruning

First you must appreciate the difference between summer fruit, which is produced on last year's wood, and autumn fruit, which is produced on new wood (i.e. the current season's). In both cases, cut back the cane to 23cm after planting and do not allow the plant to fruit the first year.

Summer raspberry pruning Cut the canes down to ground level after fruiting and tie in new growth 10cm apart to allow light and air to circulate around the plants (see Fig 104). Make sure there are no more than 7 or 8 canes to each stool, and remove all sucker growth from rows to stop overcrowding, which creates conditions favourable to disease. Most gardeners cut back the top growth of each cane during late winter or early spring; I prefer the early spring, just before the plant starts to move. The reason for this is

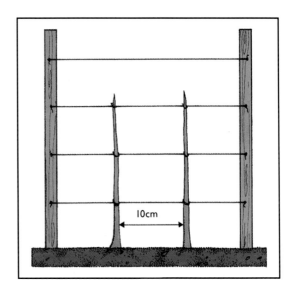

Fig 101 Spacing is an important factor.

93

Fig 102   Raspberries will need netting, but are again ideal for freezing.

because I use the top of the cane to act as protection from bad weather and frost, and if the top section were pruned before the early spring, bad weather might cause it to be cut back even further later in the spring. In early spring, therefore, cut back top growth approximately 14–16cm above the top wire.

Autumn raspberry pruning   Cut all canes down between February and March to 15cm above ground level.

Raspberry Varieties for Freezing

'Glen Clova'   Early to mid-season
'Malling Jewel'   Mid-season
'Leo'   Late season

Other Raspberry Varieties

'Lloyd George'   Early to mid-season
'Malling Orion'   Mid-season
'Norfolk Giant'   Late season

Blackcurrants

Like the blackberry, the blackcurrant is we[ll] suited to being grown organically, but unlike the blackberry, it is not allowed to produce fruit i[n] the first year. It also needs a different style o[f] pruning, since the fruit is produced on new woo[d] rather than old. Light and air must be allowed t[o] the centre of the bush to control diseases.

Soil   As described in previous chapters. Mulch throughout the growing season with a wel[l] rotted compost containing straw and F.Y.M. t[o] control weeds.

Pests and diseases   *See* Chapter 11.

Pruning   After planting, cut back to 2–3cm (i[f] not already this size when purchased), cutting t[o] a cup shape, in order to allow light and air int[o] the centre of the bush (*see* Fig 104). Later, in the autumn of the first year, cut down the weak shoots to produce stronger ones which will pro

Fig 103   Blackcurrants are full of vitamin C and store well when frozen.

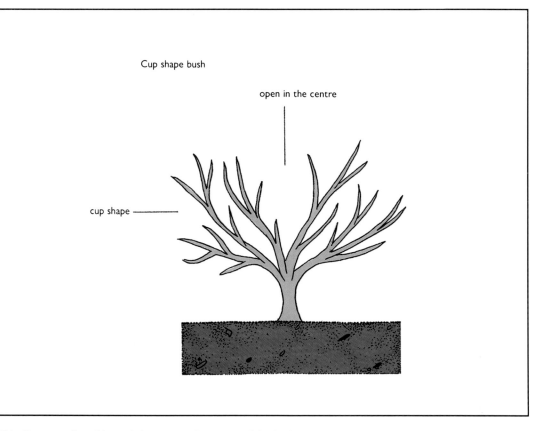

Cup shape bush

open in the centre

cup shape ──────

ig 104   Prune to allow light and air to enter the centre of the bush.

Juce the fruit in the following growing season. Annual pruning is undertaken to cut back the older wood after cropping, but remember to allow light and air into the centre of the bush throughout its life.

Blackcurrant Varieties

'Boskoop Giant'	Early season, good for freezing, rich in vitamin C.
'Cotswold Cross'	Mid-season, good for freezing, rich in vitamin C.
'Ben Nevis'	Mid to late season, good for freezing, rich in vitamin C.
'Baldwin'	Late season, rich in vitamin C, good for freezing, will produce good crop if plenty of manure is applied as recommended in Chapter 4.

Red and White Currants

The red and white currant are ideally suited to organic growing, preferring the deep cultivation described in Chapter 4. Buy two-year-old bushes and choose them with an open, cup shape.

Mulching   Cover the soil's surface with a layer of well-rotted straw containing F.Y.M.

95

Feeding Around March apply potash in the form of clean wood ash at the rate of 25–28g per sq metre.

Pests and diseases *See* Chapter 11. A fruit cage or netting is very important to prevent birds from eating fruit; windbreaks are also very beneficial.

Pruning

At all times the bush should maintain a cup shape with an open centre to allow light and air to circulate.

Winter pruning Start by removing all dead, damaged, diseased or crossing branches. The pruning that follows the three 'Ds' is done on bushes two years old or over. Cut back the branches by half to an outward-facing bud (*see* section on pruning, page 75). A form of renewal pruning to replace older growth with new may be necessary after 2 or 3 years.

Summer pruning This takes place around June, and the side branches (laterals) are cut back to 4 or 5 leaves. Summer pruning is important in order to encourage ripening of the fruits by allowing sunlight and air to reach them; it is also important in checking vigorous growth and preventing overcrowding.

Red Currant Varieties

'Jonkheer Van Tets'	Very early season.
'Laxton's No. 1'	Early season.
'Red Lake'	Mid season.
'Rivers'	Late season.
'Wilson's Long Bunch'	Late season.

White Currant Varieties

'White Grape'	Mid-season.
'White Leviathan'	Mid-season.

Gooseberries

A deep, cultivated soil with ample drainage and organic matter as described in Chapter 4 is the ideal. Those who still have problems with a clay soil should avoid varieties such as 'Careless' and 'Leveller'.

Feeding In March apply potash in the form of wood ash. The rate will depend on how much is already present in the soil.

Mulching Will help in the control of weeds.

Pests and diseases *See* Chapter 11.

Pruning

Winter and summer pruning is necessary.

Winter pruning (two-year-old bushes) As far as possible try to maintain a cup shape with an open centre which allows light and air to circulate around and through the bush. Remove any

Fig 105 Clean and look for signs of disease on gooseberries before freezing.

dead, damaged or diseased branches to stop the infection or spread of disease, and remove crossing branches to stop rubbing. Once all this has been done, cut the branches back by half to an outward-facing bud. Cut back side shoots (lateral growth) to 3 buds to encourage spurs.

Summer Pruning At the end of June cut back the side growth to 4 or 5 leaves.

Gooseberry Varieties

'Keepsake'	Early season, good for eating, cooking and freezing.
'Green Gem'	Mid-season, good for eating.
'Warrington'	Late season, good for eating and preserving.

Strawberries

Like most fruits, strawberries prefer a well-drained soil containing plenty of organic matter. Be sure to purchase certificated stock to avoid virus diseases, and if you are given runners by a neighbour or friend, check likewise.

Netting/cloches If the strawberries are out in the open, nets should be erected to prevent the birds from eating the fruit; alternatively, plants can be grown in a fruit cage. Cloches are used for protecting one-year-old plants and at the same time keep the birds off.

Pests and diseases *See* Chapter 11.

Planting *See* Chapter 7. The variety 'Cambridge Favourite' should be planted July/August.

Mulching Straw is traditionally used around the neck of the plant and outward to support the fruit, both preventing damage to the fruit and acting as a form of weed control. Plastic mats or black polythene can be used instead of straw, though these of course will not give the organic benefits of recycled straw. The area surrounding the growing section should be covered with black polythene, cutting out the light and stopping weed growth.

Extra feeding The strawberry will need plenty of phosphates and potash to produce healthy fruit, but little nitrogen in order to control the foliage. Rates will depend on the amount already in the soil. Phosphates are applied in the winter.

Strawberry varieties

'Cambridge Prizewinner'	Early season.
'Royal Sovereign'	Early season.
'Cambridge Favourite'	Mid-season, good for first-year crop, plant July/August.
'Talisman'	Mid-season.
'Rabunda'	Late season.

CHAPTER 10

Vegetables

As with other plants, it is important to choose vegetable varieties that are immune or resistant to certain diseases; however, at the end of the day we may have to accept the fact that, without the aid of chemical fertilisers, insecticides and fungicides, our crops will not always be a lush green, or totally unmarked by pests and diseases despite all our efforts and endeavours.

Drainage

Good drainage will prevent a multitude of problems, and play an important part in growing vegetables. It will influence soil temperature, producing a warm soil far earlier in the year than a soil with poor drainage, this encouraging earlier germination of seeds. The increased air flow and temperature is also helpful to the seedlings at the transplanting stage and bacterial activity in the soil is encouraged, allowing the breakdown of organic matter to accelerate. Cultivation can take place far earlier in the year, especially after heavy rainfalls.

Weather Protection

Frost and wind are the main two problems, but the odd heavy rainfall or hailstorm can also cause

Fig 106 Cloches offer good protection for plants early in the spring.

Fig 107 A greenhouse is ideal for sowing seeds in and for growing plants in during the winter.

damage to the crops. Avoid planting in a frost pocket, and erect windbreaks (*see* Chapter 11).

Growing Under Glass

Crops can be produced under glass in winter providing proper drainage and soil cultivation procedures have been followed. For the average gardener such costs as heating may outweigh the returns in crops unless growing on a large scale.

Raised Beds

The raised bed system is a good way of overcoming the drainage problem. You can have one large bed or several smaller ones, depending on the size of your garden. The practice of crop rotation is normally associated with one large bed; however, you can use 3 small raised beds or 4 if you use a system of resting a bed for one growing season.

CROP ROTATION

The aim of a three-plot crop rotation is to grow a different crop in each plot on a three-year cycle; however, there is also a four-bed system (*see* page 99). The idea, which works very well, stops the build-up of soil pests on all three plots, cultivates the soil with deep-rooting crops, and

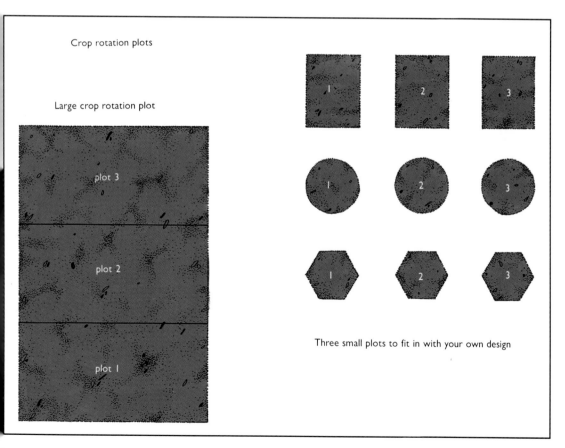

Fig 108   Crop rotation will prevent the build-up of pests and disease.

feeds the soil of each plot with the nutrients required for crops growing that year, thereby preventing contamination of the soil by a build-up of one nutrient.

Step one   Before any form of cultivation, ensure you have a good working drainage system. Cultivate the soil and bring the pH level as close to 6.5–7 as possible, as shown in Chapter 4. Raised beds can be used to provide drainage and a deeper soil.

Step two   Double dig the area or areas as described on page 36, leaving the surface layer in large lumps for the frost to break down over the winter period.

In the spring lightly fork and rake the area, working it to a fine tilth ready for sowing or transplanting.

Step three   During the winter months plan your three-year crop rotation ready for starting in the spring, as shown in the plan. (*See* page 99.)

Plot I – First year   The double digging should have been carried out in the autumn, so that sowing or planting can start as soon as the weather conditions are right.

Crop/plot I, year I   Peas, beans and all forms of salad vegetables. Remember, peas have nitrogen fixation properties. Test soil to check levels of nitrogen before adding extra organic fertilizer.

Crop/plot 2, year I   After testing the soil for nutrient levels apply a dressing of organic fertiliser such as dried blood, bonemeal and wood ash if needed.
Plant all forms of root crops.

Crop/plot 3, year I   All forms of brassicas can be grown in plot 3. They prefer a pH around 7, therefore test the soil and adjust by adding lime if necessary.

The second and third year consists of moving up one plot, i.e. the crop planted in plot I of year I, is planted in plot 2 in year 2. Plot 2 of year I becomes plot 3 in year 2 and so on, continuing in a three-year cycle.

Four-bed system

The four-bed system is basically the same as the three but one bed is allowed to remain empty for general cultivation and weed control. Sometimes these areas are planted with green manure such as mustard.

No-digging system

This is where the soil is never walked on in order to avoid compacting it, and earthworms are allowed to do most of the work, thus avoiding the need for double digging.

To follow this system you will need some form of narrow raised beds which can be in the shape of a rectangle, circle or square, whatever bests suits your garden design. The main point to remember when building the beds is that you will need to reach the centre from at least two sides. Drainage is a very important factor and is the first stage of building any form of bed; the second is cultivation of the soil to give it a good start – ensuring the pH level is correct, applying organic matter to all levels, and generally making sure conditions are right for the soil population to do its job.

Close planting

This is a system of planting the crop without spacing, therefore creating a kind of umbrella in order to stop weed growth and soil damage. However, care should be taken when following this planting system to avoid a build-up of disease caused by the lack of air flow and light. Some sections of the foliage – mainly those facing inward – may have poor growth through the lack of light and not being able to photosynthesise. A close check should also be kept on watering to avoid

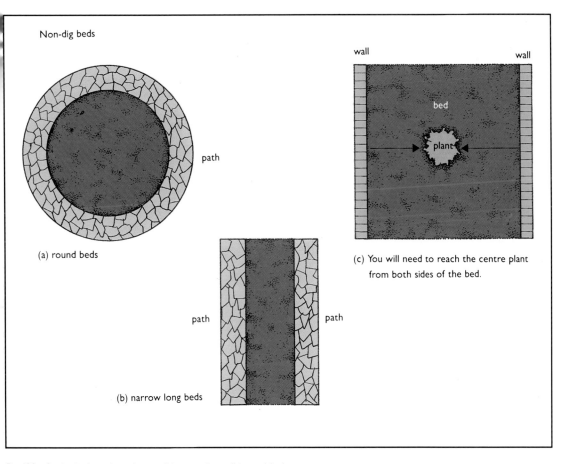

Fig 109   Beds designed so that walking on the soil is avoided.

plants drying out because of the extra competition.

VARIETIES OF VEGETABLES

It would be impossible to list all the vegetables and how to sow them; rather I have confined myself to suggesting a few varieties in each section. However, new varieties are produced yearly, and your local garden centre should be able to keep you up-to-date, especially with those which are disease resistant.

Beans

Broad bean   'Colossal', 'Imperial White Longpod', 'Imperial Green Windsor' or 'Dreadnought'. 'The Sutton' or 'The Midget' are ideal for smaller gardens.

Dwarf bean   'Sprite' or 'Tendergreen'.

Runner bean   'Achievement', 'Enorma' or 'Hammond's Dwarf Scarlet'.

Beetroot

'Crimson Globe', 'Boltardy' or 'Cheltenham Green Top'.

Broccoli

Exposed areas	'June Market', 'Reading Giant', 'Progress' and 'Thanet'.
Other	'Early Feltham', 'Late Feltham' and 'Summer Snow'. 'St Gwithian', 'St Keverne' and 'St Agnes'.
Sprouting	'Christmas Purple', 'Purple Sprouting' and 'Late White Sprouting'.

Brussels Sprouts

'Peer Gynt,' 'Rollo' and 'Sigmund'.

Cabbage

'January King Green', ready in January/February. 'Savoy Ormskirk Late', ready in late winter/early spring. 'Stockleys Red', very hardy, good for growing in exposed areas, ready autumn/winter.

Carrots

'New Red Intermediate'
'Early Nantes'
'Autumn King'

Cauliflower

Summer crops	'Classic', 'Alpha' and 'Snow King'.
Autumn crops	'Superlative', 'Autumn Giant' and 'White Chief'.
Late-autumn crops	'South Pacific' and 'Snowcap'.

Fig 110   Seeds for these carrots were sown so as to avoid the first generation of root fly.

Celery

Trench variety	'New Dwarf White', 'Unrivalled Pink' and 'Giant Red'.
Self-blanching	'Avonpearl', 'Tendercrisp' and 'Greensleeves'.

Cucumber

'Butcher's Disease Resister', 'Rocket', or the variety resistant to gummosis – 'Topsy'.

Leeks

Early varieties	'The Lyon' and 'Early Market'.
Mid season	'Musselburgh' and 'Walton Mammoth'.
Late	'Giant Winter' and 'Winter Crop'.

Fig III A simple piece of wood or some form of matting which stops cucumbers from touching the ground will prevent bruising.

Lettuce

Open, summer-grown

Cabbage (butterhead)	'Suzan', 'Cobham Green' and 'Tom Thumb'.
Cabbage (crisphead)	'Webb's Wonderful' and 'Windermere'.
Cos	'Lobjoit's Green Cos' and 'Little Gem'.
Intermediate	'Buttercrunch'.

Open, winter-grown

Cabbage	'Arctic King' and 'Valdor'.
Cos	'Hardy Winter White'.
Intermediate	'Winter Density'.

Grown under glass in winter

Cabbage 'May King', 'Kloek' and 'Unrivalled'.

Marrow

'Green Bush', 'Tender and True' and 'Custard White'.

Melon

Cantaloupe	'Ananas', 'Sweetheart' and 'Tiger'.
Casaba	'Superlative', 'Honeydew' and 'Emerald Gem'.

Mint

Apple Mint
Height   60–90cm.
Leaf colour   Pale green.

Common mint (Spearmint)
Height   60cm.
Leaf colour   Mid-green (veined).

Fig II2 Mint is easily grown and makes a useful culinary flavouring.

Mushrooms

Brown variety most resistant to disease.

Onions and Shallots

Spring sowing	'Bedfordshire Champion' and 'Wijbo'.
Autumn sowing	'Autumn Queen' and 'Solidity'.
Sets	'Stuttgart Giant' and 'Rijnsberger'.
Salad	'White Lisbon'.
Pickling	'Paris Silverskin' and 'Barla'.
Shallots	'Giant Red'.

Parsley

P. Petroselinum crispum

Use	Leaves add flavour to culinary dishes.
Recommendations	'Curly Top' and 'Green Velvet'.

Fig 113 Organically-grown onions.

Hamburg parsley

Use	Conical root developed for cooking.

Parsnip

'Avonresister' – resistant to canker, 'Offenham', 'Tender and True'.

Peas

May–June picking	'Meteor' and 'Feltham First' (round seeded). 'Kelvedon Wonder' and 'Gradus' (wrinkle seeded).
June picking	'Onward' (wrinkle seeded).
July-August picking	'Lord Chancellor' (wrinkle seeded).
September picking	'Kelvedon Wonder' and 'Pioneer', both less prone to mildew.
Mangetout	'Tall White' or 'Edward de Grace'.

Potatoes

First-early	'Sutton's Foremost'.
Second-early	'Ben Lomond' and 'Craig's Royal'.
Main crop	'King Edward' and 'Red King'.
For heavy soil	'Kerr's Pink'.

Radish

Summer radish	'Scarlet Globe', 'Red Forcing' and 'Sparkle'.
Winter radish	'China Rose'.

Spinach

'Greenmarket', 'Long Standing Round' and 'Long Standing Prickly'.

Fig 114   Developing tomatoes.

Swede

'Chignecto', which is resistant to club-root disease, 'Magnificent' and 'Western Perfection'.

Tomatoes

'Kingsley Cross', 'Ailsa Craig', 'Early Market', 'Histon Early', 'Sutton's Golden Queen'.

Turnip

'Snowball', 'Golden Ball' and 'Greentop White'.

105

CHAPTER 11

Pests and Diseases

This chapter includes suggestions for coping with adverse weather conditions. If these are followed, they will help to counteract die-back caused by frost, damage from strong winds, the loss of all your seedlings through placing them outside without hardening them off, etc.

Hygiene also plays a part, and pruning for health by allowing light and air to circulate around the plant will prevent the build-up of moulds and so make the use of chemical fungicides unnecessary.

A study of the life-cycles of pests will give you an indication of when and where they breed, and sowing can then be timed accordingly. When you know where they hide on the plant, and how to find their nest or breeding areas, you will be able to carry out pest control by hand. Places where pests might hibernate can be found and destroyed, thus helping to avoid the use of chemical insecticides.

Organic Insecticides/Fungicides

There are a few insecticides which are termed organic. These include 'derris', 'pyrethrum' and 'soapy water', and one fungicide called 'Bordeaux mixture'.

These insecticides are organic in that they are derived from plants; however, they are a form of poison which can be harmful to fish and which will kill such beneficial insects as the ladybirds that help to control aphids, and bees that are essential for pollination. Another point to consider is that since these mixtures are chemically produced, some of the chemical agents used in the process might remain in the insecticide.

Frost

All plants, whether hardy or not, will be severely damaged if attacked by frost, which causes the young growth to turn black. This 'scorching', as it is termed, may also lead to other diseases such as canker in fruit and ornamental trees. There are two kinds of frost, 'air' and 'ground', and the times when they are at their most destructive are spring and autumn. Spring frosts are the most damaging where seedlings and general planting are concerned.

Spring Frost

To understand why the spring frost may cause more damage than the autumn frost, we must first look inside the plant and see how moisture moves inside its cell system. Frost damage is caused by the moisture inside the plant's cell tissue turning into ice crystals. In the spring, most of the damage to young seedlings and plants is caused by these ice crystals in the cells warming up too quickly in the sun's rays. A traditional practice which I have found to be very helpful is to spray the plant with cold water, which slows down the warm-up period, thus causing less damage to the plant. Spraying the plant with water – watering in general – should take place before 10 o'clock in the morning and after 5 o'clock in the evening to avoid sun scorch through the droplets of water magnifying the sun's rays.

Spring frosts can occur any time from the beginning of March until the beginning of May, and it is this time when buds, new shoots and juvenile foliage run the highest risk of being damaged. Most spring frosts are ground frosts, which have a more penetrating effect than air frosts. To understand how ground frost moves, picture water running down a slope: frost will travel in a similar way, so never position plants, cold frames and glasshouses at the bottom of a slope where the frost may collect in a 'frost pocket'.

Autumn Frost

Autumn frosts are not quite so damaging as spring frosts, especially where woody plants such as ornamental trees and shrubs are concerned. This is because as the tree or shrub enters its dormancy, less and less moisture is available to form ice crystals, which also means that the tree or shrub is gradually introduced to the colder conditions of the winter months. The tree or shrub may become damaged through the autumn frost especially when a strong wind combined with a frost draws moisture from the soil around the roots of the tree or shrub. Unable to do so, the moisture which remains after dormancy is taken from the cells of the woody section and usually at the upper part of the plant.

Wind

The drying effect that a strong wind can have on the soil or seed compost, and on the woody sections, foliage and root system of a plant, can be fatal. Even plants which have a full moisture content in their cells can dry out in a matter of hours in a windy position. The reason for this is the way the plants transport moisture through their conducting cells from the root system up through to the foliage.

As shown in Fig 117, the faster the wind speed over the surface area of the foliage, the more the plant draws on the root system for moisture. If the soil or compost has dried out through the wind, the cells in the root system will collapse, which in turn leads to the collapse of the cells in the foliage, causing the whole plant to wilt, sometimes to a point beyond recovery.

The wind problem is even more serious when the soil and the cell system throughout the plant – especially woody ornamental trees and shrubs – become frozen. When this happens there is no movement of moisture in the plant. Evergreen

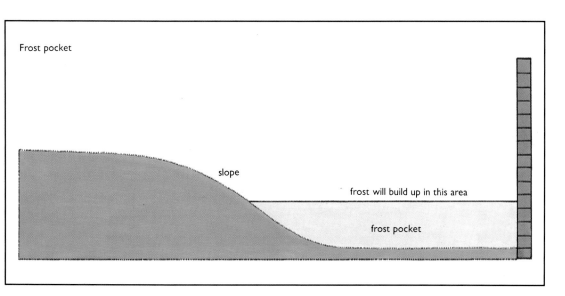

Fig 115 Avoid growing plants in frost pockets.

plants such as conifers usually turn brown. The deciduous plant, because of its dormancy and lack of foliage, is damaged by the wind drying the woody sections and making them brittle and less able to stand up to the spring frost.

Wind Control

Wind problems can be overcome by protecting the area where the plants are grown. Whilst planning your growing areas, the simple erection of canes with paper streamers tied to the top of them will give you an indication of which way the wind is channelled and of its strength. Structures such as houses, walls and fences should all be taken into consideration.

Fig 116   Wilting caused by lack of moisture.

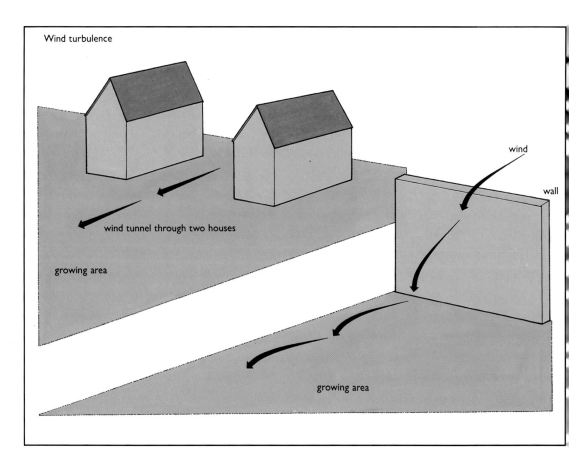

Fig 117   Avoid wind tunnels and turbulence caused by walls and fences.

Houses

Two houses close together may form a tunnel capable of producing very high wind speeds, and to site a growing area at the end of this wind tunnel would result in a reduction in crop at the very least. Corners of houses may also have a similar effect.

Walls

Solid walls will cause a turbulence as shown in Fig 117.

The damage is not caused to the growing area closest to the wall, but to the areas that catch the tail-end of the turbulence a few feet away from the wall. Therefore, erect canes with flags to establish where the most damage would be caused. If walls are planned in the open or in the centre of the garden, then an open wall which will filter wind is better than a solid one.

Fences

A fence has basically the same effect as a wall, but stands more chance of being blown over in

Fig 118   A wooden framework will offer protection by filtering the wind.

gale-force winds. It will need to be treated periodically, which may cause damage to the growing areas through droplets of chemical preservative being carried on the wind. It will also offer a hiding place with protection for over-wintering insects. Again, if it is to be erected in the centre of the garden, an open structure is better than a solid fence.

Windbreaks

Besides walls and fences there are also natural windbreaks which allow the wind to filter through and therefore avoid turbulence, for instance, hedging plants such as the conifer (Leylandii), hawthorn, beech and privet. The Leylandii is useful for ease of maintenance and speed of growth, whereas the hawthorn, which tends to be grown as an informal hedge, can look untidy in addition to playing host to many different forms of pest. The beech is very attractive, but may cause problems with scale, and the privet may be too time-consuming – it would need trimming six times a year. Whichever you choose, avoid allowing natural windbreaks to shade the growing areas.

Netting   Many garden centres sell plastic windbreaks, from small-grade mesh to large professional material. Both do the job well, and also offer some protection against frost.

Fruit cages   As mentioned in Chapter 9, a fruit cage will serve several purposes, from pest control to acting as a windbreak offering some protection against frost.

Cold frames   A very important item for the gardener who wishes to start seeds, strike cuttings and harden off plants.

Cold frames as a barrier   Certain pests such as the 'carrot root fly' have physical restrictions; by building a barrier to a height of just under a metre and enclosing the carrot seedling, the fly is unable to affect the plants. I have found that

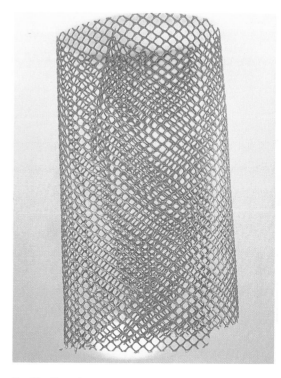

Fig 119   Greenhouse shading, or netting, also makes excellent wind-break material.

aluminium cold frames without their tops are ideal for the framework, which can be bolted together and, if need be, two or three cold frames can be used at a time. The sides can be fitted with glass or one of the heavy grade polythenes. The whole thing can be easily moved to fit in with the crop rotation programme.

Greasebands

These are used mainly for fruit growing and can be purchased from your local garden centre. However, they contain not only a sticky substance, but also an insecticide to kill the insect trapped in the grease, and it would therefore be far better to produce your own greasebands. First, cut a piece of cloth big enough to go round the trunk of the tree as shown in Fig 121. The cloth is then fastened to the tree and covered in a medical jelly. As the insect makes its way up the

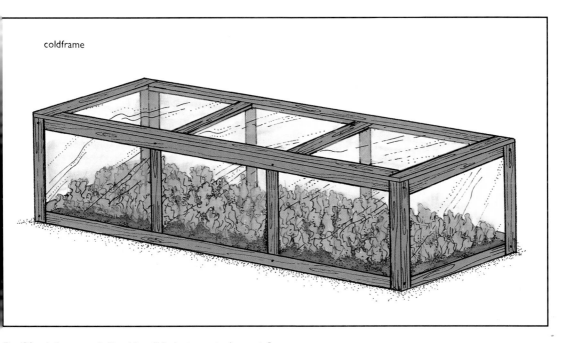

coldframe

Fig 120 A framework like this will help to control carrot fly.

trunk to hibernate for the winter, it becomes stuck in the greaseband ready for you to remove by hand.

Throughout the book I have emphasised the importance of 'natural balance' in organic gardening, and in the control of pests and diseases natural balance will play an even bigger part. Below I have listed just a few of many hundreds of insects, some of which attack our plants whilst others are beneficial. To keep a natural balance and to avoid using chemical sprays, the beneficial insects must be encouraged because they eat those insects which damage and devour our crops. Over many years of chemical spraying and as a result of the destruction of the beneficial insects' host plants or hiding places, the natural balance has been tipped in favour of the pests. Therefore, study those insects which help us and as far as possible create the conditions favourable for their breeding.

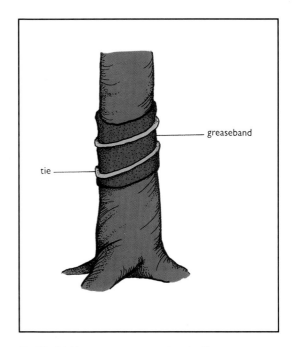

greaseband

tie

Fig 121 Making your own greaseband will avoid the need for insecticides.

HELPFUL INSECTS AND ANIMALS

Common toad	Eats slugs and insects.
Carabid beetle (*Carabus violaceus*)	Attacks aphids, slugs and snails.
Garden spider (*Meta sementata*)	Eats insects.
Hedgehog	Eats slugs and insects.
Hunting spider (*Tarentula pulverulenta*)	Eats a multitude of insects.
Hoverfly (*Syrphus balteatus*)	Aids pollination and helps to control aphids.
Ichneumon fly (*Ichneumon sp*)	Lays eggs in the larvae of moths, beetles and aphids.
Lacewing (*Chrysopa carnea*)	Attacks caterpillars and aphids.
Ladybird (*Coccinella septempunctata*)	Eats aphids.
Parasitic fly (*Dexiosoma caninum*)	Helps to control cockchafers (maybugs).
Parasitic wasp (Apantales *glomeratus*)	Helps to control white caterpillars and aphids.
Predaceous capsid (*Anthocoris nemorum*)	Feeds on scale insects aphids and spider mites.
Sail wasp (*Ophion sp*)	Lays eggs in the larvae of other insects.

PESTS

Further reading to keep you up-to-date with new forms of control can be purchased from the Ministry of Agriculture, though most of these will be based on chemicals. You can, however, skip the chemicals section and instead study the insects' life cycles.

Adelgids *(Adelgidae)*

How they attack	Sap-suckers, the young feed on base of new leaves.
What they attack	Mainly conifers.
Description	Black or dark brown, covered in a white waxy wool, 1–2mm long.
Signs of attack	Honeydew, sooty moulds, galls and other malformations.
Life cycle	*Adelges abietis* overwinter on spruce trees and start to mature in the spring when the females lay eggs. The young hatch in a few weeks and feed on the base of new leaves, which then develop to form pineapple galls. The galls break open in August/September and new flying adelgids emerge to move on to another host plant.

Aphids *(Aphididae)*

Common name	Greenfly, blackfly and blight.

Rosy Apple Aphid *(Dysaphis plantaginea)*

How they attack	Sap-suckers, they infest blossom and leaves.
What they attack	Apples.
Description	Pink to grey, covered in a white waxy powder.
Life cycle	*See* Green apple aphid.

Green Apple Aphid *(Aphis pomi)*

How they attack	Sap-suckers.
What they attack	Apples and pears.
Description	Yellow-green to bright green with dark brown siphunculi.
Life cycle	Eggs are about 0.5mm long and black. Hatch from mid-

Fig 122   Aphids, also known as greenflies, cause great damage to plants.

March and the young feed on leaves and blossom trusses. Rosy apple aphid lay eggs in September/October-early November.

Woolly Aphid *(Eriosoma lanigerum)*

How they attack	Sap-suckers, the young feed on twigs and branches.
What they attack	Apple, cotoneaster and hawthorn trees.
Description	Small, brown and covered in woolly wax.
Life cycle	Overwinter in cracks and galls, feed of branches, spurs and wounds from March. By the autumn, breeding stops and aphids seek shelter for the winter.

Pear-Bedstraw Aphid *(Dysaphis pyri)*

How they attack	Sap-suckers, they infest new growth.
What they attack	Pear trees.
Description	Pink or pink-brown covered with white mealy wax.
Life cycle	Eggs which were laid in the autumn hatch in the spring (and are often found on fruiting spurs) before transferring to bedstraw in late spring.

Peach-Potato Aphid *(Myzus persicae)*

How they attack	Sap-suckers, they feed on the new growth of peach trees.
What they attack	Peach trees, potatoes, lettuce and tomatoes, as well as many flowering and ornamental plants.
Description	Pale yellow to green and pink.
Life cycle	Eggs overwinter on peach trees and start to hatch as the temperature rises. Winged aphids develop in May which carry virus diseases and transfer to different plants.

Blackcurrant Aphid *(Cryptomyzus galeopsidis)*

How they attack	Sap-suckers, they attack young new leaves.
What they attack	Blackcurrants.
Description	Greenish-white.
Life cycle	Eggs overwinter and hatch as the buds develop. Winged aphids develop and lay eggs in the autumn.

Black Bean Aphid *(Aphis fabae)*

How they attack	Sap-suckers, they feed on young leaves.
What they attack	French, runner and broad beans.
Description	Black.
Life cycle	Shiny black eggs are laid next to buds in the autumn. They begin to hatch in April. *This aphid carries bean yellow mosaic virus.

Cabbage Aphid *(Brevicoryne brassicae)*

How they attack	Sap-suckers, the young feed on new leaves.
What they attack	Cabbage, swedes and brussels sprouts.
Description	Green-grey covered with a white mealy wax.
Life cycle	Eggs overwinter on leaves and stems, hatching out in April. The young eat new leaves, flower stalks and buds. From May–July, aphids fly to younger plants and new eggs will be produced in the autumn. *This aphid carries cauliflower and turnip mosaic viruses.

Pea Aphid *(Acyrthosiphon pisum)*

How they attack	Sap-suckers.
What they attack	Peas.
Description	Yellow, pink or pale green.
Life cycle	Eggs overwinter on trefoils and clovers, winged aphids develop from May. *This aphid carries bean yellow mosaic and pea-leaf roll.

Water-Lily Aphid *(Rhopalosiphum nymphacae)*

How they attack	Sap-suckers, they feed on leaves and flower buds.
What they attack	Water-lilies.
Description	Brown or dark green.
Life cycle	Overwinter on Prunus and fly to aquatic plants in summer.

Caterpillars

Fruit Tortrix Moths

How they attack	Feed on fruit and leaves.
What they attack	Apples, plums and pears.
Description	Green caterpillars about 2.5cm long.
Life cycle	Eggs laid on leaves on which the caterpillar feeds for

caterpillar damage

Fig 123 Remove caterpillars by hand.

about a month (in spring).
Cocoons spun, caterpillars
pupate and second batch of
adults appears in autumn,
laying eggs which will
develop in spring.

Magpie Moth (Abraxas grossulariata

How they attack	Feed on leaves.
What they attack	Currants and gooseberries.
Description	White, yellow and black caterpillars.
Life cycle	Eggs laid on underside of leaves in late summer and caterpillar feeds until autumn. Overwinters in leaf litter, bark, etc until April. Cocoons spun, black and yellow moths appear in July-August.

Cutworms

How they attack	Eat stems, usually at night.
What they attack	Lettuce, potatoes and carrots.
Description	Vary between grey-brown to green or yellow.
Life cycle	Eggs laid on leaves in mid summer, which, when hatched, the caterpillar feeds on for a couple of months. After pupating, these caterpillars emerge in August/September and overwinter in soil.

Cabbage Caterpillar

Large White Butterfly (Pieris brassicae) or Cabbage White

How they attack	Feed on host plant.
What they attack	Cabbage.
Description	Hairy black and yellow caterpillars, up to 5cm long.

Life cycle	Eggs laid on leaves in April–May which hatch about two weeks later. The caterpillar feeds on plant for about a month before pupating. Adult emerges between July and August and further eggs are laid early September. Further adults can emerge from these eggs, although most overwinter to produce adults in spring.

Tomato Moth (Lacanobia oleracea)

How they attack	Feed on leaves.
What they attack	Tomatoes and cucumbers.
Description	Brown to yellow-green caterpillars.
Life cycle	Eggs laid in May/June on underside of leaves which caterpillar eats when hatched Caterpillar pupates on plant debris, walls, etc and adult emerges about two weeks later. Between July and September, pupae develop and overwinter.

Yellow Potato Cyst Eelworm (Globodera rostochiensis)

How they attack	Roots infested.
What they attack	Potatoes and tomatoes.
Description	Yellow, white or shiny brown cysts about ½cm long.
Life cycle	Eggs within dead female hatch when host plant nearby. Roots send out chemical messages to eggs, and young transfer to roots where female grows, fertilised by male eelworms, and the cysts then lie in soil. Eelworm can multiply very quickly.

Flies

Pear Midge (Contarinia pyrivora)

How they attack   Feed inside young fruit.
What they attack   Pears.
Description   White-yellow larvae.
Life cycle   Larvae overwinter under pear tree and develop in spring. Females fly up to lay eggs in unopened flowers in April/May. Young feed on developing fruit and either fall with fruit to ground or leave before to overwinter.

Leatherjackets (Daddy-long-legs)

How they attack   Feed on stems and roots.
What they attack   Strawberries, cabbage and seedlings.
Description   Larvae are grey-brown.
Life cycle   Adults emerge and mate at the end of August/September. Eggs are laid near plants in soil and larvae feed on them until pupating at the end of the following summer. They particularly like warm, damp summers.

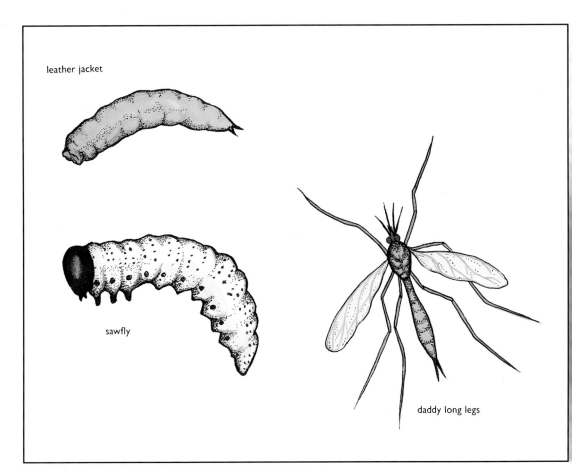

leather jacket

sawfly

daddy long legs

Fig 124 Troublesome insects.

Carrot Fly (Psila rosae)

How they attack	Feed on roots.
What they attack	Carrots, parsley and parsnips.
Description	Larvae creamy-white, up to lcm long.
Life cycle	Larvae and pupae over-winter and adults emerge in May/June. White eggs laid near host plant in soil on which the larvae feed before pupating. Second generation of adults emerges in August/September which will pupate and overwinter.

Onion Fly (Delia antiqua)

How they attack	Feed on stems and bulbs.
What they attack	Onions, leeks and shallots.
Description	White maggot.
Life cycle	Eggs laid on leaves and stems. When hatched the maggots eat the host plant before travelling to the soil to pupate. Cycle is repeated during the summer and the final pupae remain in the soil to overwinter before emerging as following year's adults.

Apple Sawfly (Hoplocampa testudinea)

How they attack	Eat young fruit.
What they attack	Apples.
Description	Larvae creamy-white.
Life cycle	Eggs laid in spring in open blossom. As blossom falls, eggs hatch and young burrow into fruitlet. This they eat, then continue to a second fruitlet. Eventually, larvae drop to soil, spin cocoons and overwinter.

Pear Sucker (Psylla pyricola)

How they attack	Sap-suckers, the young feed on buds and new growth.
What they attack	Pears.
Description	Wide bodies and prominent eyes.
Life cycle	Eggs laid in March on shoots and spurs which young feed on. Three generations emerge during year and final one overwinters.

Pea Thrips (Kakothrips pisivorus)

How they attack	Feed on leaves and flowers, causing silvering of leaves.
What they attack	Pea pods and broad beans.
Description	Brown-yellow adults and yellow larvae.
Life cycle	Adults emerge in late spring and fly to plant. Eggs laid in stamens which hatch within a week. Young feed for 2–3 weeks before going back to the soil for winter protection. At their worst June/July.

Ants

Not too much of a nuisance; however, leaves are occasionally eaten though seeds are more commonly stolen and taken to nest.

Beetles

Chafers

How they attack	Adults sometimes eat leaves.
What they attack	Lawns, potatoes and raspberries.
Description	Brown, grey or black, normally with hard covering.
Life cycle	Eggs laid in soil during summer close to host plant. Larvae then eat roots and will

continue to develop for 1–5 years.

Colorado Beetle (Leptinotarsa decemlineata)

How they attack	Feed on leaves.
What they attack	Potatoes.
Description	Orange-yellow eggs laid on underside of potato leaves and larvae then feed for about a month. Move to soil to pupate and by autumn all adults move to soil to over-winter.
	Should a beetle or out-break be discovered, Ministry of Agriculture must be informed.

Flea Beetles

How they attack	Leaves and roots eaten.
What they attack	Cabbage, turnip and swede.
Description	Striped.
Life cycle	Adult beetles emerge in spring to feed on young leaves after overwintering in plant debris. Eggs laid near host plant in soil during May/June and once hatched larvae feed on plant. Adults feed until October, before overwintering.

Vine Weevil (Otiorhynchus singularis)

How they attack	Roots eaten.
What they attack	Gooseberries, raspberries and apples.
Description	White, up to 8mm long, no legs.
Life cycle	Eggs laid in soil close to host plant and once hatched feed for about 3 months before

pupating. Cannot fly, but adults transfer to new areas by the transfer of plants and by crawling.

Wireworms

How they attack	Feed on roots.
What they attack	Potatoes, cabbages and strawberries.
Description	White to yellow, up to 2.5cm long, tough skin.
Life cycle	Eggs laid June/July in soil, feed for up to 5 years. Adults emerge from pupae stage late summer/early autumn but remain in cell until following summer before mating. Main feeding times March–May and September/October.

Potato Capsid

How they attack	Sap-suckers.
What they attack	Potatoes.
Description	Green.
Life cycle	Eggs laid in July/August which hatch in the following May/June.

Common Froghopper (Philaenus spumarius)

How they attack	Sap-suckers.
What they attack	Raspberries and black-berries.
Description	Small green insect, frog-like in appearance, usually covered in froth or 'cuckoo spit'.
Life cycle	Eggs laid in autumn in herbaceous plants or stems, hatching the following May. Young mature by July and lay eggs for overwintering.

Fig 126   Red spider will increase in numbers during hot, dry weather.

Fig 125   Cuckoo spit, or the 'froghopper', can be seen in abundance on some plants, but to see the insect you have to look under the bubbles, or as in this case, wait until they emerge.

Spotted Millipede *(Blaniulus guttulatus)*

How and what they attack	Occasionally eat seeds or seedlings, but generally feed on dead plants.
Description	Pale yellow with red spots running down sides of body.
Life cycle	Eggs laid on soil surface during spring and summer. Young resemble adults but with fewer segments.

Fruit Tree Red Spider Mite *(Panonychus ulmi)*

How they attack	Sap-suckers.
What they attack	Pears, apples and plum trees.
Description	Eggs red-brown, about 0.15mm round. Adult red-brown.
Life cycle	Eggs hatch April–June and the young feed on underside of leaves and can produce four further generations in one year. When temperature drops, eggs are laid to overwinter.

Slugs and Snails

Field Slug (Deroceras reticulatum)

How they attack	Eat leaves of live or dead plants.
What they attack	Some fruit and most vegetables.

119

Description	Fawn or light grey, about 3–4cm long.
Life cycle	*See* Garden snail.

Garden Slug (Arion hortensis)

How they attack	Some fruit and most vege-tables.
Description	Black or dark grey.
Life cycle	*See* Garden snail.

Garden Snail (Helix aspersa)

How they attack	Feed on leaves.
What they attack	Some fruit and most vege-tables.
Description	Shell brown-grey, up to 3cm across.
Life cycle	Eggs laid in soil or cavities in spring, hatching about a month later. Some lay eggs in autumn which will hatch in spring.

Wasps

More of a nuisance factor than actually harmful. Can extend damage already caused by other pests.

Woodlice (Oniscus asellus)

How they attack	Feed on leaves and seed-lings, but largely on decaying matter.
What they attack	Cucumbers, amongst other plants.
Description	Brown-grey, hard bodies up to 2cm long.
Life cycle	Once eggs are hatched, young feed for several months before maturing. Prefer damp conditions.

Fig 127 Snails feed more on debris than on the plant itself.

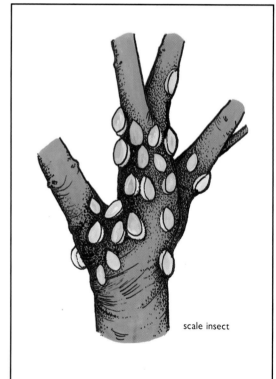

scale insect

Fig 128 Scale insects can be removed by hand.

DISEASES

Cankers

Apple and Pear Canker (Nectria galligena)

What it affects	Apples and pears.
What to look for	Shows itself in several different ways such as papery bark; a cream-coloured pustule growth in the spring, turning red during the winter; and branches dying back close to the affected area.
Cure	Clean out the canker back to clean wood using a wire brush.

Coral Spot (Nectria cinnabarina)

This fungus will attack almost the complete range of woody plants, causing die-back. It will even-tually either kill the tree or bush, or cause the shape to be changed because of the drastic pruning measures that have to be taken. Once the plant has been attacked by this fungus there is always the danger that it will return and put other plants at risk. In bad cases, therefore, it is probably best to destroy the plant by burning.

Coral spot is recognised by its salmon-pink coloured growths about the size of a pinhead (see Fig 129).

Die-back

Many types of plants suffer from die-back in one form or another. This may be caused by fungi and bacteria leading to forms of canker; scale insects, which also help to introduce fungi into the

Fig 129 Coral spot can be fatal, therefore never leave stumps.

Fig 130 Black leaves caused by frost. (Pruned areas should be covered to avoid die-back.)

plant; viruses; frost damage; wind; bad pruning; and many other things, all adding to the confusion. Therefore, when coming across die-back, look for the cause, which may be other than on or in the diseased plant. Make notes and use the experience in the future; never say, 'It's just one of those things that happens to plants'; and remember, prevention is better than cure.

Control As a general rule to cover all die-back, remove diseased branches, cutting back into clean wood. Never keep the prunings – burn them or put them in a plastic bag until such time as burning is convenient – which should be no longer than a week.

Lettuce Downy Mildew *(Bremia lactucae)*

What it affects	Lettuce.
What to look for	Yellow or pale green areas on upper side of leaf with whitish mould underneath.
How it works	Spores in soil from previously diseased crop.

Onion Downy Mildew *(Peronospora destructor)*

What it affects	Onions and shallots.
What to look for	Off-white turning to purple mould on dead parts. Leaves turn yellow and fall.
How it works	In autumn, airborne spores infect bulb where fungus overwinters. In spring, spores transfer to young plants.

Apple Powdery Mildew *(Podosphaera leucotricha)*

What it affects	Apple trees (and pears to a lesser degree).
What to look for	White, powdery coating on leaves and flowers. Flower

and leaf fall, often leaving odd leaves at end of branch.

How it works	Infection carried by wind in summer from fungus produced in previous autumn. Buds often survive and are primary source for following year.

Strawberry Powdery Mildew *(Sphaerotheca macularis)*

What it affects	Strawberries and occasionally other 'berries'.
What to look for	Grey-white, powdery patches on underside and dark red blotches on upper side of leaf.
How it works	Infection spread by wind.

Rots/Grey Mould *(Botrytis cinerea)*

This disease usually follows damping off disease found with seedlings, but it will attack buds and

Fig 131 Grey mould and other forms of mould can be fatal to seedlings, therefore you should always use a clean pot and fresh soil.

cause die-back on woody sections of some plants. The disease is recognised by its grey, fluffy mould growing on the affected area.

Control Avoid over-watering especially when temperatures are low, and ensure free drainage of seed trays and pots. Space out seed trays and prune plants to allow light and air to circulate freely, taking out crossing branches.

Rusts

Blackberry Stem Rust (Kuehneola uredinis)

What it affects	Blackberries and loganberries.
What to look for	Yellowish spots on leaf surface and underside as well as on canes.
How it works	Spores germinate on leaf and the rust overwinters.

Leek Rust (Puccinia allii)

What it affects	Leeks and onions.
What to look for	Reddish-orange, dusty pustules on leaves and stems.

Plum Rust (Tranzschelia discolor)

What it affects	Plum trees.
What to look for	Yellow spots on upper surface of leaf and brown, powdery patches underneath in July. During course of year, patch underneath leaf turns black and the leaf can turn yellow and drop off in severe cases.
How it works	Spores germinate in spring and affect anemones — which in turn reinfect plum trees.

Glossary

Acid soil A soil which has a pH of below 7.0.

Aeration Free passage of air within the soil.

Alkaline soil A soil which has a pH of above 7.0.

Annual Plant which germinates, grows and sets seed in one season, thus completing its life cycle.

Anther Part of the stamen within the flower which contains pollen.

Apex Tip or top of stem.

Aquatic plant Plant which grows in water.

Bedding plant Plant used for temporary spring and summer display.

Biennial Plant which grows in the first year, flowers and sets seed in second year.

Bleeding Sap exuded when a cut is made in a plant.

Broadcast Scattering of fertiliser or seed over a wide area.

Bud Point from which new growth extends.

Bulbil Small bulb which grows on stem or base of bulb.

Catch crop Crop which grows either between maturing plant and one just planted or between a slow-growing and a quick-growing plant.

Chlorosis Yellowing appearance caused by lack of chlorophyll.

Clone (Clonal) Identical plant grown vegetatively (i.e. by cuttings) from the original parent plant.

Compost a) Well-rotted material used as a soil conditioner which also offers forms of nutrients in small amounts.

b) A mixture of growing mediums such as loam, sand, etc, used for sowing seed (seed compost) or potting on (potting compost).

Cordon Plant (usually fruit tree) trained to grow as a single stem.

Corm A swollen modified stem base, bulb-like in appearance. Shoots grow from bud at top.

Cotyledon First set of leaves produced by seedling. Usually bear no resemblance to final shape of leaf.

Damping down Adding water to surface of bench, pathway, etc, to create a humid atmosphere around aerial section of plant, particularly useful in warm weather.

Deciduous Plant which loses its leaves in dormant season.

Dicotyledon Plant which has two seed leaves.

Dormant The state of being inactive, period when plant growth and manufacturing processes close down.

Earthing up The practice of drawing earth up to shelter plant from light, e.g. when growing potatoes.

Espalier Plant (usually fruit tree) which is trained to have a vertical trunk and branches at 30–40cm intervals.

Evergreen A plant which retains its foliage throughout year.

F_1 hybrid Obtained when two closely-related seed strains are crossed.

Forcing a) The practice of encouraging a plant to develop faster than its natural rate, or

b) To start a plant artificially from a dormancy.

Fruiting body Fungus, i.e. mushrooms and bread mould.

Fumigate To disinfect (a glasshouse) using smoke or gas containing a fungicide or an insecticide.

Fungicide A chemical solution used to kill fungus.

Genus Category which identifies a 'family' within the botanical world, i.e. all maples belong to the *Acer* family.

Ground cover Plants which cover soil surface, preventing light and moisture from reaching unwanted plant-growth.

Half-hardy Plants which must be protected from frosts.

Half Standard Plant (usually tree or shrub) with single stem usually 75–120cm before branches.

Hardening off Process by which plants are acclimatised over a period to outdoor or cooler conditions after propagation under glass or in sheltered positions.

Hardy Outdoor plants which will tolerate colder conditions of winter.

Herbaceous A plant which does not form a woody stem.

Humus Brown, glue-like substance derived from the breakdown of vegetation and animal by-products.

Hybrid Two plants from distant species which are crossed to form a new variety.

Inorganic The use of synthetically produced artificial chemicals rather than those derived from natural sources.

Insecticide Chemicals used to control and kill insects.

Insectivorous Plants which catch insects to use as food from which to obtain minerals.

Internode Distance between one leaf node to the next.

Larva Young of butterflies, moths, etc.

Lateral Side branch which grows from main stem.

Leaching Soluble matter drawn through soil by water and gravity.

Leader Leading branch of plant.

Leaf Mould Partially decayed leaves which break down to form a brown, flaky mass.

Maiden Young grafted tree in its first year (nursery term).

Marginal plant One requiring plenty of moisture, best grown at edge of pool in shallow water.

Monocotyledon Only one seed leaf.

Mulch Layer of straw, leaf mould, etc, around plants which helps retain moisture, keeps weed growth down and protects low-growing fruit such as strawberries.

Mutant Plant or part of plant which does not conform to standard.

Naturalising Plants allowed to grow informally in natural conditions, e.g. daffodils and other bulbs.

Nectar Sweet liquid produced by plants and in flowers that attract insects, which play a vital role in pollination.

Node Point from which leaves and branches grow.

Nymph Young of aphids, etc.

Organic Natural substances obtained from the breaking down of plant or animal remains.

Oxygenator A plant submerged in water and producing oxygen.

Pan i) Condition of the soil where heavy watering or rain has caused hard packing of the surface.
ii) Hard layer of soil caused through mechanical cultivation to the same depth each time.
iii) A shallow pot used to grow seedlings.

Parasite Something which lives off a host plant and is incapable of independent existence.

Peat Substance naturally formed from vegetable remains in wet areas such as bogs.

Perennial Plant which lives indefinitely, such as herbaceous plants.

pH This refers to the percentage of hydrogen ions in the soil; the pH scale enables one to measure acidity levels and determine the type of soil. Neutral stage is 7.0, soil above this point is alkaline, below 7.0 it is acidic. Soil-testing kits can be obtained from garden centres and once soil type is established suitable plants can be chosen accordingly.

Pollard Practice of cutting trees hard back to main trunk. Willow trees respond well to this treatment, but most garden trees should be chosen with their eventual height in mind in order to avoid such drastic measures.

Pricking out The planting out of seedlings into larger containers or individual pots. This is only done when they have produced their first set of adult leaves.

Pupa Also known as chrysalid, the stage between larva and adult in butterfly and moth families, etc.

Remontant Plant which flowers more than once during year.

Resting period Dormancy period when plant puts on little or no growth.

Rhizome Underground stem from which roots grow.

Rogue Similar to mutant, an atypical plant.

Root run Area used by roots of plant.

Rootstock A plant into which a second plant is grafted.

Saprophyte Plant which gains nourishment from decayed organic matter.

Scion Branch or bud which is transferred to a second plant by grafting.

Seedling Young plant.

Self-compatible Plant which does not need pollinating by second plant.

Self-fertile Plant which does not need pollinating by another plant.

Self-incompatible Needs a pollinator, or in some cases two, to produce fruit.

Self-sterile Needs a pollinator, or in some cases two, to produce fruit.

Species Type of plant which always grows true to form.

Sphagnum Type of moss which has good water retention facilities.

Spore Tiny reproductive 'cells' of such plants as mosses and ferns, also of some diseases.

Spur Lateral branches which produce sub-laterals bearing several flower buds.

Sterile Not producing seeds.

Stigma Section of flower which produces sticky fluid for reproduction.

Stolon Branch or stem which grows horizontally and produces roots at nodes, thus producing further plantlets.

Stool Term used for trees and shrubs which are pruned close to ground annually.

Stopping The removal of the growing tip of a plant to encourage the production of lateral branches.

Strain Plant from a species which is grown by seed.

Stratification Process used to overcome dormancy in seeds of hardy plants which need a cold period before germination. These are planted in a pot in sandy soil and left in a sheltered position outside or in a coldframe in winter. Stratification can take place during summer by placing seeds in the fridge.

Style Stalky section connecting ovary of flower to stigma at top.

Tap-root Main anchoring root of plant.

Terminal Usually referring to buds, branches or flowers found at the tip of a stem or branch.

Tilth Crumb-like texture of surface soil, ideally suited to seed sowing.

Top-dressing Addition of fresh soil, or organic fertiliser to the surface of the soil.

Trench Soil dug out up to a depth of 1 metre for deep-rooting crops.

Tuber Swollen stem or fleshy root growing underground.

Under-plant Small plants grown under and around larger ones.

Unisexual Flower containing only female or only male sex organs, not both.

Variegated Leaves which have more than one colour.

Weed Plant which is growing where it is not wanted.

Index